Twayne's English Authors Series

Sylvia E. Bowman, *Editor*

INDIANA UNIVERSITY

W. S. Gilbert

TEAS 178

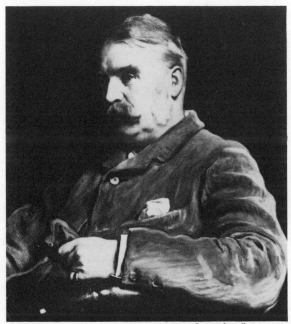

Painting by Frank Holl, R.A., 1886
Photo courtesy of The National Portrait
Gallery, London

W. S. Gilbert

W. S. Gilbert

By MAX KEITH SUTTON

Department of English
University of Kansas

TWAYNE PUBLISHERS

A DIVISION OF G. K. HALL & CO., BOSTON

Library of Congress Cataloging in Publication Data

Sutton, Max Keith.
  W. S. Gilbert.

  (Twayne's English authors series ; TEAS 178)
  Bibliography: p. 139-45.
  Includes index.
  1. Gilbert, Sir William Schwenck, 1836-1911.
I. Title.
PR4714.S87   828'.8'09   74-23984
ISBN 0-8057-1217-8

MANUFACTURED IN THE UNITED STATES OF AMERICA

66952

For
Claire, Stephen, Julia, and Katherine

Contents

About the Author

Max Keith Sutton holds the B.A. from the University of Arkansas and the M.A. and Ph.D. from Duke University. He has written articles on Victorian humor and satire and on works by Robert Browning, Christopher Smart, and R. D. Blackmore. Since 1964 he has taught at the University of Kansas, where he is now an Associate Professor of English. Dr. Sutton's current research is in British and American pastoral writing of the nineteenth century.

Preface

W. S. Gilbert "pursued the mind of his day into its fantasies." This statement in the *Times Literary Supplement* on the hundredth anniversary of Gilbert's birth leads to the obvious, though often challenged view, that he is primarily a satirist — a special one who invites a change of attitude toward serious fantasies by exposing them in a comic light. In the dreams that he explores, one basic concern is the conflict between individual impulse and some form of law. While this conflict is by no means limited to "the mind of his day," Gilbert's treatment of it needs to be seen in its Victorian context, where particular goals, anxieties, and compulsions can be identified. Much of his social and literary context has been illuminated by Reginald Allen's introductions in *The First Night Gilbert and Sullivan,* by Leslie Baily's *Gilbert and Sullivan Book,* and by the work of Jane Stedman: her dissertation and her edition of Gilbert's German Reed plays give a detailed picture of his place in the Victorian theater, where popular dreams and illusions often took their most extravagant form.

Because Gilbert wrote over seventy works for the stage, as well as many short stories, prose sketches, verses, and reviews, this study is not centered upon the fourteen operas produced in collaboration with Arthur Sullivan. These form his most significant body of writing, but they are not the only wheat among the chaff of an overproductive career. His nearly forgotten pieces sometimes attain satiric excellence; they often clarify his central concerns; and they must be remembered if we are to realize his range and industry as a writer. The three main sections of this study are meant to suggest the size and proportions of three areas of Gilbert's work: the first chapter deals with his early journalism; the second treats his start as a dramatist and his plays without Sullivan in the 1870's; the third focuses upon recurrent themes and patterns of action in the operas.

Because thematic connections are often more important than order of composition, my approach is only roughly chronological. But I have followed the main outline of Gilbert's literary career from 1861, when he began contributing to *Fun*, to his death in 1911. Thanks to Reginald Allen's *Anniversary Survey*, Gilbert's work in these five decades can be clearly kept in mind. Though he began writing plays in the 1860's, his main work in this decade was journalistic, and it culminated in the publication of *The Bab Ballads*. In the 1870's, his busiest period as a playwright, he began the partnership with Sullivan; the 1880's were the golden years of their prosperous collaboration. After their estrangement in 1890, Gilbert achieved no marked popular success in either the two last operas with Sullivan or the libretti he wrote for two other composers. His last decade was peaceful and mostly non-productive, but he had a brief flash of creativity shortly before he died.

For assistance in conducting research, I am indebted to Mr. Herbert Cahoon of the Pierpont Morgan Library; to the staffs of the Lilly Library at Indiana University, the New York Public Library, and the British Museum; and to the inter-library loan departments of the University of Kansas, the University of Minnesota, and the Toronto Public Libraries. My work has received financial support from a Watkins Summer Fellowship and research grants from the University of Kansas. Professor Ray L. White of the University of North Carolina at Raleigh gave generous help at the start of this project, and since then I have become indebted to many helpful people, especially to John Bush Jones for guidance in the difficult field of Gilbertian bibliography; to James Helyar for technical aid; to Bill and Nan Scott for sharing their books, recordings, and critical appreciation of Gilbert and Sullivan; and to my wife, Claire, for much practical help and encouragement, and for showing me the drama of choice in *Iolanthe*.

MAX KEITH SUTTON

University of Kansas

Chronology

1836   William Schwenck Gilbert born November 18, at 17 Southampton Street, Strand, London; the son of William Gilbert, a recently retired naval surgeon who later became a novelist, and Anne Morris Gilbert.

c.1839 Kidnapped at Naples and ransomed for twenty-five pounds. Acquired the pet name of "Bab."

1842   Attended school at Boulogne.

1846 - Attended Western Grammar School, Brompton.
1849

1849 - Attended Great Ealing School; became head boy at sixteen.
1852

1853   Entered the Department of General Literature and Science, King's College, University of London.

1855   Entered the Inner Temple as a student of law.

1857   Received his Bachelor of Arts from the University of London (Gilbert dates this a year earlier in "An Autobiography"). Passed a competitive examination for a clerkship in the Education Department of the Privy Council Office. Began two decades of service in the militia.

1858   Appeared in print for the first time with his translation of the laughing song from Auber's *Manon Lescaut* in the program for the Promenade Concerts.

1861   Inherited three hundred pounds; resigned clerkship; began contributing to *Fun*, the new rival of *Punch*.

1863   Called to the bar. "My Maiden Brief" published; *Uncle Baby* produced. Began "The Comic Physiognomist" in *Fun*.

1865   Contributed briefly to *Punch*.

1866   Wrote *Dulcamara*, the first of his five operatic burlesques in the 1860's. Published "The Yarn of the Nancy Bell" and many parody reviews in *Fun*. Joined northern circuit as a

	barrister; earned only seventy-five pounds in two years. Began illustrating his father's novels.
1867	Married Lucy Agnes Turner, August 6. Began publishing *Bab Ballads* regularly in *Fun*. Wrote *Harlequin Cock-Robin and Jenny Wren* for the pantomime season.
1868	Became a drama critic for the *Illustrated Times*. Prepared *Bab Ballads* for publication.
1869	Met Arthur Sullivan. Productions: *No Cards* (the first of his six pieces for the German Reeds' Gallery of Illustration); *An Old Score*; and *Ages Ago* with music by Frederic Clay.
1870	Productions: *The Princess*; *The Gentleman in Black*, with music by Clay; *Our Island Home*, with music by German Reed; and *The Palace of Truth*. Went to Paris as war correspondent for *The Observer*.
1871	Productions: *Randall's Thumb*; *A Sensation Novel*, with music by German Reed; *Creatures of Impulse*, with music by Alberto Randegger; *Great Expectations*; *On Guard*; *Pygmalion and Galatea*; and *Thespis* (December 26), his first "grotesque" opera with music by Sullivan.
1872	Production: *Happy Arcadia*, with music by Clay.
1873	Productions: *The Wicked World*; *The Happy Land*, written in collaboration with Gilbert à Beckett as parody of *The Wicked World* and satire of Gladstone's cabinet (the play was censored by the Lord Chamberlain); *The Realm of Joy*; and *The Wedding March*. Published *More Bab Ballads*; unsuccessfully sued the *Pall Mall Gazette* for calling parts of *The Wicked World* indecent.
1874	Productions: *Charity*; *Ought We to Visit Her?*; *Committed for Trial*; *Topsy-Turvydom*; and *Sweethearts*. Published "Rosencrantz and Guildenstern," his last contribution to *Fun*.
1875	Productions: *Trial by Jury* (March 25), his first success with Sullivan; *Tom Cobb*; *Eyes and No Eyes*; and *Broken Hearts*. Began his association with the impressario Richard D'Oyly Carte.
1876	Productions: *Princess Toto*, with music by Clay; and *Dan'l Druce*. Tried to mediate between his estranged parents.
1877	Productions: *On Bail*; *Engaged*; and *The Sorcerer* (November 17). Published *Fifty Bab Ballads* and a reply to a personal attack by Miss Henrietta Hodson, an actress and the manager of the Royalty Theatre.
1878	Productions: *H. M. S. Pinafore* (May 25), which made the

partnership famous; and *The Ne'er-Do-Well*. Resigned from the militia.

1879 Productions: *Gretchen*; and *The Pirates of Penzance* (December 31), with music by Sullivan. Went to New York with Sullivan to produce the authorized *Pinafore* and *The Pirates*.

1880 Formed touring companies in America; returned to England for the London production of *The Pirates*.

1881 Productions: *Foggarty's Fairy*; and *Patience* (April 23), the opera which was moved in October to Carte's new Savoy Theatre for Gilbert and Sullivan.

1882 Production: *Iolanthe* (November 25), with music by Sullivan.

1883 Submitted the "Lozenge Plot" to Sullivan, who rejected it. Signed a new five-year contract with Carte and Sullivan.

1884 Productions: *Princess Ida* (January 5), with music by Sullivan; and *Comedy and Tragedy*. Tried to sustain Sullivan's flagging interest in writing comic opera. Proposed the "Lozenge Plot," which was again rejected. Proposed the plot for *The Mikado*. Revised *The Sorcerer* for revival with *Trial by Jury*.

1885 Productions: *The Mikado* (March 14), with music by Sullivan.

1887 Production: *Ruddygore* (January 22: the spelling was changed later as a polite gesture). Proposed the "Lozenge Plot" again without success.

1888 Supervised revivals of *The Pirates* and *The Mikado*. Completed his most serious libretto for Sullivan, *The Yeoman of the Guard* (produced October 3). Resolved to write no more serious plays after failure of *Brantinghame Hall*.

1889 Turned down Sullivan's request for a grand opera libretto. Completed *The Gondoliers* for him instead (produced December 7).

1890 Began the "carpet quarrel" over Carte's handling of finances; withdrew from the partnership and successfully brought legal action against Carte. Persuaded Alfred Cellier to write music for the "Lozenge Plot." Moved to Grim's Dyke. Published *Foggarty's Fairy and Other Tales*.

1891 Became deputy lieutenant of the County of Middlesex. Published *Songs of a Savoyard* with dedication to Sullivan.

1892 Productions: *Mountebanks*, with music by Cellier; *Haste to the Wedding*, with music by George Grossmith, Jr. Agreed to a new contract with Sullivan.

1893 Production: *Utopia (Limited)* (October 7), with music by

Sullivan. Was appointed justice of the peace for the division of Gore in Middlesex.

1894   Production: *His Excellency*, with music by Osmond Carr.

1896   Production: *The Grand Duke* (March 7), the last opera with Sullivan.

1897 - Assisted in revivals of operas at the Savoy. Traveled exten-
1911   sively; was in Egypt when Sullivan died on November 22, 1900. Wrote *The Fortune-Hunter* (1897); *The Fairy's Dilemma* (1904); *Fallen Fairies* (1909), with music by Edward German; and *The Hooligan* (1911). Was knighted in 1907. Protested the banning of *The Mikado* during the state visit of Prince Fushimi, but later testified in favor of the principle of stage censorship. Died of heart failure after coming to the aid of a woman in the pool at Grim's Dyke (May 27, 1911); his ashes buried at Great Stanmore Church, Middlesex.

1919   The D'Oyly Carte Opera Company began a London season.

CHAPTER 1

The Emergence of a "Doggerel Bard"

W S. GILBERT began adulthood with a shift from romantic expectation to real tedium. At King's College, London, in 1855, he plunged into the study of ballistics, hoping to serve as an artillery officer in the Crimean War. But the war ended before he was ready; and, instead of fighting the Russians on heroic battlefields, the young man found himself in 1857 beginning four years of "detestable thralldom" as an assistant clerk in the Education Department of the Privy Council.[1] Fettered to this "baleful office" at one hundred and twenty pounds a year, Gilbert worked in a humdrum world where heroism at best consisted of the easy-going endurance of Anthony Trollope's Johnny Eames or the forlorn independence of Herman Melville's Bartleby. Service in the militia soon added variety to the young clerk's life, and he came to realize his good fortune in avoiding Russian bullets and all the other perils of an ordeal by battle. But his twenty years as a peace-time soldier could never invest him with the heroism that he saw in the veterans returning from the Crimea:

As they marched through great towns in their tattered uniform, with bearskins and shakoes half shot away, their faces bronzed, and covered with ragged beard; and, above all, their colours shot off almost to the pole, carried by dirty ragged lads, who still somehow looked like gentlemen . . . as these sturdy warriors tramped through the English towns they had little expected to see again, women went into hysterics, and strong men, after shouting themselves hoarse with a kind of mad welcome that let itself go free to take what form it would, threw themselves down upon the grass, and there lay prone, and wept like women.[2]

This ungainly sentence from an early short story was Gilbert's way of paying tribute to heroes. But heroism was something that he saw only at a distance, and he wrote far more succinctly when treating his own militia experience as a source of humor. By 1864, he was caricaturing himself as a bumbling, self-important, militia man at the Guildford maneuvers;[3] and some of the sharpest lines in the Savoy operas depict the vanity, not the grandeur, of soldiers:

> When I first put this uniform on,
> I said, as I looked in the glass,
> 'It's one to a million
> That any civilian
> My figure and form will surpass.'[4]

Having missed his chance for romantic adventure (and an early death in a Crimean hospital), Gilbert learned to make a career of showing the comic differences between prosaic experience and the ideals and expectations of romance.

A more crucial move toward finding a profession was his second false start — his four futile years as a barrister. With the three hundred pounds left to him by an aunt, he resigned his clerkship in 1861 ("the happiest day of my life")[5] and paid one hundred pounds for his call to the bar; he was admitted in November, 1863.[6] This move was a natural one, for Gilbert had begun his legal studies as an undergraduate, and it was to become significant in terms of his later attitudes and actions. Just as his military training points toward his punctiliousness as a stage director, his experience as a barrister anticipates the habits of the dramatist who constructed his libretti "like so many briefs."[7] In personal relationships, his early interest in the law foreshadows his legalistic approach to conflicts throughout his adult life. Though Gilbert abandoned the profession after four lackadaisical years, he never dropped the lawyer's habit of collecting evidence, especially for use in his own defense. If he possessed the satirist's eye for injustice, his vision was keenest when injustice struck closest to home; that is, at himself. His typical strategy was to document the offense in an effort to receive a verdict in his favor. If nothing else, the evidence and the verdict were to prove to the world that he was a wronged man.

I   *The Importance of Law in Gilbert's Life and Work*

Gilbert's role as a plaintiff-at-large begins early and lasts long in his career. One of his first publications is a letter to *The Times*, written when he was twenty-three and expressing just resentment against some bullying Guardsmen — military anti-heroes unlike the veterans from the Crimea. The letter documents a personal affront in the interests of all pedestrians who face similar perils on the London streets: "Early on Sunday morning, as I was proceeding along the south side of Knightsbridge-road, a little east of Sloane-street, I met three Guardsmen walking arm-in-arm with as many women. I gave them a wide berth, but one of the fellows deliberately came up to me and struck me violently on the chest with his elbow. The blow sent me staggering into the road in a most undignified manner."[8]

After this touch of self-directed humor, Gilbert stays curiously formal in narrating the action: "I seized the man, and informed him that I should detain him until I saw a policeman." The report is as calm as the testimony of an ideal witness who tells of the scuffle, of the subsequent attempt to hit him with a belt "in true Guardsman style," and of the flight of the bullies when a passerby came to Gilbert's assistance. Then he broadens the seriousness of the assault by reporting an earlier fracas in which two Guardsmen "nearly killed one policeman" and "severely injured another, besides wounding some of the passers-by, with their belts." He ends by suggesting a remedy for this public nuisance: "If the authorities object to turning the men into the streets without their belts (and it must be allowed that a beltless soldier presents a very slovenly appearance), let the belt be stitched firmly to the tunic at the back. . . ." Seen in retrospect, the letter reveals the traits of an ideal satirist: sensitivity to injustice, boldness in combatting it, a sense of humor, and the ability to propose a remedy for a bad situation.

Throughout the biography by Hesketh Pearson, Gilbert's sensitivity to personal injustice is a recurrent motif. The grievances range from a sum of thirteen pounds and three shillings, which he felt was due to him from the first publisher of *The Bab Ballads*, to the "very distressing noise" made by his neighbor's servants when raking out cinders,[9] and eventually to the discovery that he and Sullivan were charged five hundred pounds for new carpets at the Savoy Theatre.[10] Sooner or later, Gilbert voiced his stock response: "I shall place the matter at once in the hands of my solicitor."[11] When wronged, he sought reparations and public apologies like the one from Arthur à Beckett, the editor of the *Tomahawk* (Pearson suggests that it was dictated by Gilbert himself): "I . . . am bound to declare that Mr W S Gilbert has treated me with the courtesy befitting a gentleman. I gladly withdraw all and every imputation I made against him at the time when I imagined him guilty of an action of which I now firmly believe him to be incapable."[12]

In his legal disputes, Gilbert made an issue of his own integrity. It was perhaps never challenged more bitterly than when Miss Henrietta Hodson (married to another of Gilbert's enemies, Henry Labouchere) publicly accused him of slander and other forms of persecution. As an actress and as the manager of the Royalty Theatre, Miss Hodson summarized her grievances in a pamphlet relating "*The Persecutions She Has Suffered from Mr. William Schwenck Gilbert*" (April, 1877). She suggested that he would stoop at nothing to achieve a public vindication. Referring to a letter of praise by J. B. Buckstone, which Gilbert had copied in self-defense, she wrote: "YOU ARE FULLY CAPABLE OF EITHER HAVING DICTATED IT TO HIM OR OF HAVING FORGED IT TO SUIT YOUR OWN PURPOSES."[13]

Gilbert dealt with this charge by printing it in capitals, to show that Miss Hodson was the victim of what would later be called a persecution complex. The passage formed one segment of his elaborately documented *Letter Addressed to the Members of the Dramatic Profession in Reply to Miss Henrietta Hodson's Pamphlet* (May, 1877). Gilbert had the last word in this controversy, just as he later did in the "carpet quarrel" with Richard D'Oyly Carte and Arthur Sullivan.[14] Contrasted with Miss Hodson's outrage, the judicial tone of Gilbert's *Reply* almost creates a reversal of roles in which Gilbert changes from oppressor to suffering victim. "I assume that there is a limit to the amount of abuse which a dramatic author is called upon to submit to at the hands of an actress," he wrote, "and I take it that in the paragraph I have quoted that limit is overstepped."[15] From his viewpoint, he appears to be the justified plaintiff against the persecutions of Miss Henrietta Hodson.

This pamphlet war and his years of litigation do not prove that he acted only to protect his ego. On the contrary, his first letter to Sullivan during the "carpet quarrel" expresses concern for his partner's rights as well as his own.[16] His efforts to mediate between his separated parents in 1876 shows him intent upon achieving some bearable arrangement that would protect his father from unnecessary discomfort; the only defensive note in his published letters to his mother during this crisis occurs when he resists taking any blame for what happened: "I have nothing more to add, except that your statement that you appealed to me to prevent the impending separation is, as you are well aware, absolutely untrue."[17] But he reveals in every conflict a compelling need to feel himself in the right. The strength of this need appears two years after the "carpet quarrel" when he construed in his letters from Sullivan a terrible reflection upon "my honour and good faith." Only after Sullivan responded by professing utter faith in Gilbert's honesty did he confess that by "dwelling on the subject day and night I have magnified it to the proportions of a nightmare" (Nov. 15, 1892).[18]

Gilbert's tendency to brood over some slight to his integrity appears in his letters to Clement Scott, the drama critic who reported F. C. Burnand's jest about Gilbert's serious play of 1875, *Broken Hearts*, which Burnand called "Broken Parts."[19] Though Gilbert's letters to Scott in 1877 and 1879 show his effort to salvage their friendship, he could not ignore this offense after Scott compounded it with a harsh review in 1888 of another serious play, *Brantinghame Hall*. Near the end of Scott's life, Gilbert wrote him one of the curtest birthday greetings on record: "Nor do I think that the fact that you will have achieved sixty years on the 6th October is a reason for a general jubilation. I am sixty-five, and nobody seems to care. I bear no ill-will toward you, but I have an excellent memory."[20]

Through his memory and his file of letters documenting grievances, Gilbert must have felt some satisfaction as well as self-pity. He could play the game which Eric Berne calls "Now I've Got You" with a reasonable assurance of winning.[21] But the price of victory was alienation from old friends and the disruption of his partnership with Sullivan, who steadfastly refused to give him credit in the "carpet quarrel" for being even technically right.[22] The need to win technical victories forms a more appealing theme in his comic works than it does in his biography. His ridicule of legalistic attitudes suggests a strong projective element in his satire — something comparable to Charles Dickens the moralist who attacks "the moral Pecksniff" and Thackeray the compulsive gambler who exposes the wastrel Barry Lyndon. But, unlike Gilbert, his characters find legalism more of a hindrance than a help. "Deuce take the Law!" says Nanki-Poo in *The Mikado* (Act I), expressing the typical frustration of a comic young lover who confronts a legal barrier — his father's law against flirting. Gilbert illustrates Northrop Frye's assertion that "the action of comedy . . . is not unlike the action of a lawsuit," and that it often develops in response to "some absurd, cruel, or irrational law."[23]

But not only the young lovers complain, for even the Lord Chancellor in *Iolanthe* chafes at legal restraints. Although "the Law is the true embodiment/Of everything that's excellent," it torments him with professional scruples against marrying his own ward. "Ah, my Lords, it is indeed painful to have to sit upon a woolsack which is stuffed with such thorns as these!" (Act I). Laws — against flirting, against marrying a mortal, against marrying two wives at a time — provide a basis for Gilbert's comic plots; and such legal barriers become so restrictive that they almost bring the action to a standstill, as in *Trial by Jury*, or threaten the fairies in *Iolanthe* with mass slaughter.

The plots are unraveled not by defying the law but by discovering a way to be technically right. "The subtleties of the legal mind are equal to the emergency," says the Lord Chancellor, who suggests that the Fairy Law be altered: "Let it stand that every fairy shall die who don't marry a mortal, and there you are, out of your difficulty at once!" This dénouement, echoed by the ingenious reasoning at the end of *The Mikado* and *Ruddigore*, offers a verbal resolution to the clash between external restraints and personal desires. By making the resolution so artificial, Gilbert suggests the absurdity of relying upon legalism to solve human conflicts. Given his use of the law in his personal battles, he could hardly create a satiric implication that would strike closer to home.

Gilbert's concern with legality is only part of his larger concern with the unwritten laws of social and literary convention. According to A. H. Godwin, convention is the main target of his satire.[24] In its effect upon the civilized person, a rule of decorum could be just as binding as a law made in Parliament. The weight of such rules was especially heavy in the great decade of middle-class propriety, the 1860's, when Gilbert began writing.[25] His characters move about with an inner mechanism of prohibitions and commands: "Do not speak until you are spoken to"; "Do your duty"; "Make your heart your only guide"; "Do not love someone whom you like — at least don't be selfish enough to marry a lovable person"; "Do not say damme." Gilbert's satire against this burden of restrictions appears most clearly in *Utopia Limited* (1893) when Lady Sophy instructs the native girls in the rules of English courtship:

> English girls of well-bred notions
> Shun all unrehearsed emotions.
> English girls of highest class
> Practice them before the glass.

Her lecture is a late refinement of Mrs. Grundy's teachings at the start of the century; it comes close to the advice of Mrs. General in Dickens's *Little Dorrit* (1857): "Father is rather vulgar, my dear.

The word Papa, besides, gives a pretty form to the lips. Papa, potatoes, poultry, prunes, and prism, are all very good words for the lips: especially prunes and prism. You will find it serviceable, in the formation of a demeanour, if you sometimes say to yourself in company — on entering a room, for instance — Papa, potatoes, poultry, prunes and prism, prunes and prism" (Book II, Chapter V). Because Lady Sophy and Mrs. General would make each person completely unspontaneous, their advice could become the most tyrannical of unwritten laws.

Gilbert's rationale for Victorian propriety is expressed directly in lines he added to his adaptation of Jacques Offenbach's comic opera, *Les Brigands* (1871). In the opera, the bandit chieftain enforces convention, telling his romantic daughter that "in the present artificial condition of society we cannot afford to listen to the promptings of nature. That which is natural is always unbusiness-like."[26] If this aphorism is meant seriously, we can understand why Gilbert spoke of "that charnal house, Society," in "Haunted" (*Fun* [Mar. 24, 1866], 12). By opposing nature, society deadens human life. From his viewpoint, social restraints invite hypocrisy, the repression of feeling, and stereotyped speech. His satires exaggerate and ridicule the repressiveness of society, normally without presenting any clear alternative to it; but his serious plays dramatize the need to escape from conventional behavior. In *Ought We to Visit Her?* (1874), the heroine, Mrs. Theobald, feels stifled by English provincial life; as a former actress trying to assume a role in society, she expresses convincing impatience with falsehood: "I know that I like reality," she says, in lines which Gilbert closely adapted from the novel of this title by Annie Edwards; "sham made-up speeches have no effect on me. I've heard too many of them on the stage." (Gilbert added the slam at the Victorian theater.)[27]

As the plaindealer who tries to "speak straight out from the heart" (Act I), Mrs. Theobald illustrates the socially dangerous honesty which Gilbert saw in himself in his letter to Clement Scott, (March 8, 1877): "I always speak openly, without fear or favour — & I am quite incapable of an act of social treachery."[28] But because she is open, her cautious husband must ask her to use "the stereotyped phrases of civilized life" if she wants acceptance in "this damned neighborhood" of respectable Chalkshire.[29] Ultimately, Mrs. Theobald decides that the price of respectability is too high and retreats with her husband to the Continent where she can live by the principle which Gilbert later formulated in *Utopia Limited:*

> Whatever you are — be that:
> Whatever you say — be true:
> Straightforwardly act —
> Be honest — in fact,
> Be nobody else but *you*.
> (Vol. II, 344)

This verse may be Gilbert's most positive statement of his values, but the tone suggests a problem for a writer who would like to affirm his values in a comic mode. Unlike Lady Sophy's lecture, these lines are not comic; nor are the two Utopian princesses as amusing in responding to this advice as they were when they mimed the lesson in English social decorum. Mrs. Theobald is not comic in her struggle to be free, nor are the heroines of Gilbert's other serious plays — *Pygmalion and Galatea* (1871), *Charity* (1874), and *Gretchen* (1879) — where each makes painful decisions with a sense of full responsibility. Gilbert's humor depends upon his vision of how compulsively people can behave — how even when exchanging clerical propriety for a reckless course of croquet, smoking, flirting, and dancing, the Reverend Hopley Porter of "The Rival Curates" welcomes being forced into his freedom:

> "For years I've longed for some
> Excuse for this revulsion:
> Now that excuse has come —
> I do it on compulsion!!!",
> (*Fun*, Oct. 19, 1867, 57.)

If Henri Bergson is right in saying that "All that is serious in life comes from our freedom," then the comic must come from our compulsive behavior and our occasional resemblance to puppets.[30] Much of Bergson's comic theory applies directly to Gilbert, whose characters display mechanistic habits and, in *The Mountebanks* (1892), even become clockwork dolls. But his comedy is not based upon Bergson's assumption that society is organic rather than mechanistic in its workings and that it values free, spontaneous behavior over conformity. "Society will . . . be suspicious of all inelasticity of character,"[31] according to Bergson; but Gilbert implies that the dominant powers — Mrs. Grundy and Lady Sophy — fear elasticity, because it makes people unpredictable and hard to control. Honesty disrupts society in *The Palace of Truth* (1870); for social success inside the palace depends upon possessing a talisman which gives one the power to go on lying.

While Bergson assumes that the "living society" has more power than the mechanistic elements within it, Gilbert's work suggests that the vital society can be nearly smothered by the artificial. For the vital elements to survive, lip service must at least be paid to the controlling powers: the law must be revised, not broken; the Mikado's egotism must be gratified, not defied: "your Majesty's will is law." Even the Utopian princesses become liberated by following a new rule in place of Lady Sophy's: they keep within bounds as securely as Hopley Porter; and, in their naive acceptance of a new authority which commands them to be free, they perhaps stay compulsive enough to be comic after all.

From the start of his career, Gilbert seemed to know that the law had some primal connection with humor. Legal processes have a marked ritualistic quality, especially in England; and, as Bergson points out, wherever there is ceremony there is also "a latent comic element. . . . Everyone knows how easily the comic spirit exercises its ingenuity on social actions of a stereotyped nature, from an ordinary prize-distribution to the solemn sitting of a court of justice."[32] Gilbert turned naturally to a courtroom in one of his first extended comic works, the story entitled "My Maiden Brief" which appeared in the *Cornhill Magazine* in December, 1863. Though *Fun* (the new rival of *Punch*) had been printing his hackwork since 1861,[33] publication in the *Cornhill*, a magazine founded by Thackeray, must have fed Gilbert's literary ambitions — and all the more because his piece appeared in an issue containing installments of Elizabeth Gaskell's *Cousin Phillis* and of Trollope's *Small House at Allington*, and two poems by Alfred Tennyson. The story seems to depict Gilbert's blunders as a barrister; but, according to the *Dictionary of National Biography*, his call to the bar took place less than a month before the story was published, and his biographers are probably inaccurate in treating it as an event in his life.[34]

The humor of "My Maiden Brief" is directed against a fictitious narrator, Horace Penditton, who reports his humiliation in trying to defend a pickpocket at the Old Bailey. Encouraged by his "indispensable other self," Felix Polter, Penditton accepts his first case, agrees to follow the line of defense suggested by Polter, and invites his friends to their chambers for a dress rehearsal, hopeful of success the next day. The trial becomes a matter of ceremonial importance to the narrator; he shaves his "flourishing moustache" to look more proper; and he comes forth in his gown, wig, and a pair of gold spectacles: "I looked the sucking bencher to the life."[35] He proves ready to sacrifice everything about himself (including his nagging fear that the case is impossible) for the chance of winning social approval in the courtroom. The trial will be his rite of passage into respectable society.

But the "latent comic element" of ceremonial life is "only waiting for an opportunity to burst out into full view."[36] In the formal setting of Old Bailey, the real Horace Penditton masquerades in wig and gown (Bergson's "mechanical encrusted upon the living"), and finds himself to be an impostor instead of an initiate. His friend Polter turns traitor, accepting the place of the absent counsel for the prosecution; and he easily tears down the defense which Penditton had carefully learned from him. Stunned by this betrayal, the narrator can only go through the motions of defending his client, a surly Mrs. Briggs. He reports the sad result of cross-examining the policeman who had discovered the purse in her pocket:

"Did you find anything else?"
"Yes, sir."
"What?"
"Two other purses, a watch with the bow broken, three handkerchiefs, two silver pencil cases, and a hymn book." (*Roars of laughter*).
"You may stand down." (731)

After the verdict, Penditton suffers his worst humiliation: "No sooner had the learned judge pronounced this sentence than the poor soul stooped down, and taking off a heavy boot, flung it at my head. . . . The boot missed me, but hit a reporter on the head, and to this fact I am disposed to attribute the unfavorable light in which my speech for the defense was placed in two or three of the leading daily papers next morning" (732).

The comic element bursts out with the violence of the pickpocket's anger, upsetting courtroom decorum and the pretense that people are as rational and sober as the occasion requires. Her outburst deprives the narrator of his last vestige of dignity, though he clings to it by blaming the ill-aimed boot for the sorry picture of himself in the morning papers. Despite his exposure, he remains incorrigibly image-conscious, waiting for a second brief, while Polter, having proven himself as a barrister, gives up writing farces and becomes a flourishing Old Bailey counsel.

II *Finding a Persona*

Finding a profession remained a problem for Gilbert during the first half of the 1860's. Not only was he leading a double life as a hopeful, though indolent, barrister and as a busy comic journalist, but he was filling half-a-dozen different roles within his second profession. He was supplying *Fun* with cartoons, art criticism, reviews of plays, prose sketches, verses, and "Gossip of the Week";[37] he began sending features to *Punch*; and he submitted short stories to magazines and Christmas annuals. One of his stories, published in 1866, offers a detailed glimpse of what the life of a young barrister, journalist, and aspiring dramatist must have been like: " . . . we were dramatic authors, Maxwell and I. Of course we were a great many other things besides, for dramatic authorship in England is but an unremunerative calling at the best of times; and Maxwell and I were mere beginners. We wrote for magazines, we were dramatic critics, we were the life and soul (such as they were) of London and provincial comic papers, we supplied 'London Letters,' crammed with exclusive political secrets, and high-class aristocratic gossip, for credulous country journals; we wrote ballads for music publishers, and we did leaders and reviews for the weeklies."[38]

With such a multitude of demands, Gilbert faced the prospect of continually fragmenting his energies. The situation could foster a lifetime of hackwork. *Fun* called for fragments — pen and pencil sketches, short verses, and jokes; Gilbert seldom wrote anything longer than two columns (he was paid by the inch).[39] But in these unpromising circumstances he eventually learned to create one unifying element in his work. This element is his comic persona, "Bab," whose distinctively absurd viewpoint emerged in the second half of the decade as a new facet of Victorian humor.

In Gilbert's early contributions to *Fun*, no distinctive style and viewpoint mark his work as his own. Very little of it before 1865 can be definitely attributed to him, and the drawings signed "W. S. G." or "Bab" did not invariably illustrate his own writings.[40] Until he signed himself consistently "Bab," he was essentially an anonymous humorist who filled "Gossip of the Week" in *Fun* with items like this one, which he dredged up two decades later as an example of a bad joke in *The Yeomen of the Guard*: "CALAMITOUS ACCIDENT. — A poor, thoughtless old gentleman sat down, the other day, on the spur of the moment. His screams were frightful" (December 19, 1863, 138).

The verses attributed to Gilbert from this period show few signs of his ironic viewpoint in *The Bab Ballads*. In two illustrated poems of December 12, 1863, a cattle show is seen first from the aristocratic and then from the proletarian point of view. To express the attitudes of contrasting groups became one of Gilbert's tasks as a librettist, but his verses in *Fun* do not point forward to his more immediate role as the creator of stylized absurdity in *The Bab Ballads*. His illustrations do, however: regimented aristocrats bow in unison, schoolboys march by in lock-step, a gentleman gazes through his pince-nez at a pig. At the bottom of the page, the shilling crowd is equally stylized as it crushes toward the center of the picture in a mass of leaning figures. Apparently Gilbert's talent for simplifying and stylizing experience first developed in his graphic art. The drawings express a comic vision; the verses report an event without offering a view of its latent absurdity.

In another early work ascribed to Gilbert, the comic viewpoint is again stronger in the illustration than in the jingling verses which chronicle the sights and sounds of Derby Day, 1864. The drawing is fantastically stylized, with angular figures — sometimes doubled or even tripled — pressing against one another. The lines are so sharp and numerous that the sketch almost vibrates. The verses also give an effect of motion and rising excitement, but the speaker does little more than report his impressions; he does not create a view of the silliness of the Derby Day crowd. The poem is a strange kind of reportorial art, a tolerant contrast to Hippolyte Taine's shocked response to Derby Day in 1862 — "the beast is unleashed."[41] Gilbert's poem is still readable, but not for its humor so much as for its impressionistic record of social history.

Recording impressions was one of Gilbert's basic tasks during his first five years with *Fun*. He moved toward a more active role when he began criticizing what he saw — a new painting at the Royal Academy, a new play, or a personage of London life, sketched and analyzed from the viewpoint of his first major persona, the Comic Physiognomist. Assuming this role was an important step toward greater freedom as a humorist. The series of sketches by the Comic Physiognomist began in November, 1863 and lasted — with several interruptions — until May, 1867, when the "C. P." announced his marriage. (Gilbert married Agnes Turner in August of that year.) The subject of the series is as much Gilbert's comic persona as the traits of the characters whom he brutally analyzes. Except for the cryptic epigraph — " 'Ha,' quoth Panurge" — the series begins dismally (November 7, 1863). The puns are frequent and pointless; the mock erudition has no function except to display the narrator's basic trait — unbridled egotism. Using the premise that the "acute physiognomist will possess a handsome appearance," he invites absolute trust: "as greatness and goodness are combined in our person in an unprecedented degree, modesty must necessarily be found also. That being placed beyond a doubt, we have no hesitation in assuring our readers that they may place the fullest confidence in everything we have to say on the subject of physiognomy, for we are very beautiful" (*Fun*, November 7, 1863, 78).

The Comic Physiognomist thus becomes the vehicle for a central comic theme. Egotism preoccupied Gilbert as much as it did George Meredith, and his journalistic personae swell with a sense of infinite self-importance. The "C. P." is first cousin to Gilbert's Art Critic who claims that slow music accompanied his tour of the Royal Academy; and he is like Gilbert's aspiring humorist who signs himself "A Trembling Beginner," after making an outrageous prophecy in *Fun* which in some ways came true: "Am I destined to revolutionize the árt of comic writing? Am I the man who is to write the burlesques and extravaganzas of the future? Are managers of theatres and editors of light literature doomed to fall prostrate at my feet in humble obeisance? Is it to me that society at large must look for its amusement for the next (say) forty years? To these questions I unhesitatingly reply 'I am! They are! It is!' " ("The Art of Parody," September 9, 1865, 169).

Such fantasies of power and adulation represent the driving spirit of Gilbert's comic personae. The "C. P." asserts that a mass cult has sprung up around him, that the "Maidens of England"[42] all want to marry him, that millions of disciples "have worshipped at his poor feet" (January 30, 1864, 202). His disciples become so numerous, in fact, and such a nuisance — seizing a man by the head to examine his teeth or pursuing some human specimen with a butterfly net — that the "C. P." feels certain that the Lord Mayor will suppress the series. His manic conceit supplies Gilbert's central irony: a man who is blind to his own limitations pretends to instruct others in the understanding of human character. When the "C. P." begins to describe people, the shallowness of his interests prevents much life from coming into Gilbert's writing. Hardly any of the people have names; their speeches are seldom recorded; they have the faintest sort of identity. Each description is a meager Theophrastan "Character," a thin echo of the seventeenth-century work by Sir Thomas Overbury and by John Earle, but nothing in Gilbert's prose rivals their brilliance and copiousness of metaphor. While Gilbert must have relied upon his drawings to add substance to his prose, his work hardly bears comparison with its model in Victorian character writing. Thackeray's "Snob Papers" had appeared in *Punch* some twenty years earlier and had revealed what might be achieved in this vein of comic journalism. Gilbert alludes to these papers in his last series in *Fun* by misquoting Thackeray's definition of a snob and then quarreling with it: he thought that Thackeray had said that a snob "meanly imitates" instead of "meanly admires mean things" (March 23, 1867, 22). Gilbert is equally inattentive in learning from the master's portrayal of people; for, unlike Thackeray's, his characters never come alive; he allots each one so little space that there is no room for the conversation that makes Thackeray's Captain Spitfire memorable, as he illustrates political snobbery while talking at his club: " 'Why wasn't the Princess Scragamoffsky at Lady Palmerston's party, Minns? Because *she can't* show — and why can't she show? Shall I tell you, Minns, why she can't show? The Princess Scragamoffsky's back is flayed alive. Minns — I tell you it's raw, sir!' "[43]

By contrast, the Comic Physiognomist exhibits his characters as if they were captured specimens. His club man, a milder counterpart of Captain Spitfire, is reported to us and catalogued; he is not represented as a personality in action: "This rather important old gentleman, with the semi-bald head, the over-hanging eyebrows, and the full white whiskers, is a member of the Senior United Service Club. He is an old Navy Post-Captain of the better class of the old school. Not one of the grog-drinking, swearing, indelicate old martinets of naval novels and naval plays, but a gentlemanly, fussy, obstinate, honourable, crotchetty, courteous old boy . . ." (April 6, 1867, 43). For the "C. P.", this portraiture is sympathetic, but it does not bring the subject close to us: the elderly captain exists in outline, with an attached listing of his mannerisms and opinions.

Above all else, the "C. P." keeps his distance from his subjects. Despite his boast that "In every soul he recognizes a man and a brother, save and except those only in whom he identifies a woman and a sister" (July 9, 1864, 165), his normal attitude is condescending if not scornful. Individuality does not easily catch his attention. Among the vagabonds at Epsom Downs, where he spends a night in a gypsy's tent, he discovers that the gypsy women who run the booths "are all alike — as much alike as babies" (*ibid.*). He lacks the impulse to understand the lowly characters whose histories had been recorded by Henry Mayhew in *The London Labour and the London Poor,* which Gilbert helped illustrate when it was published as *London Characters* in 1870. Low life irritates the fastidious "C. P." At the Old Bailey, he sees "the nastiest crowd in England" (July 23,

1864, 185); and he seems rather pleased that the pickpocket, the robber, the begging-letter swindler, and the "swell mobsman" are getting their just desserts. Only one man, a miserable embezzler, with a respectable looking wife, arouses his sympathies.

At a music hall he reaches a peak of irritability. There the "patron or aristocrat" is "horrible" — "a bloated, beer-sodden young man of two-and-twenty or so, covered with flash jewellery, and as supercilious in his demeanour as he is unwholesome in complexion. . . . He stands cigars and rum and water to every official who wants it (and they nearly all do), and considers the comic lady a stunner" (July 16, 1864, 182). The narrator finds her ghastly: "Such a combination of impudence, effrontery, incapacity, and utter unwomanliness the C. P. never yet had the misfortune to encounter. . . . This lady was a supreme favourite, and was encored five times." The last sentence reveals the extent of the "C. P.'s" alienation: his is the one sneering face in the entire audience.

At such moments the Comic Physiognomist shows his kinship with another of Gilbert's personae, the "Snarler," who signs the columns entitled "Out-of-Town Talk" and "Our Own Correspondent" in *Fun* during 1865 and 1866. In these reports, irritability becomes professed misanthropy; and the Snarler's viewpoint leads at times to some of Gilbert's most direct satire. Because the Snarler includes himself in his misanthropic vision, Gilbert avoids one temptation of the Victorian satirist: the creation of so respectable a bond between the persona and the reader that no one feels involved in the faults under attack. Gilbert sometimes falls into this temptation, as in his account of the criminals on the London streets, where "you and I" are contrasted smugly (or very ironically) with the parade of embezzlers, forgers, and roughs who threaten respectable society.[44] But the Snarler can implicate everyone. On his way to gamble at Spa, he asserts that social prohibition, not conscience, prevents crime. "The pleasure of doing wrong is enormous"; and, when it is encouraged "by an enlightened Christian government[,] its attractions are positively irresistible" (October 14, 1865, 49). The argument foreshadows Hopley Porter's eagerness to lead a rakish life "on compulsion" ("The Rival Curates," 1867): but Gilbert extends it toward more disturbing matters than croquet and smoking: "At a gambling watering place, the best of us become gamblers, and if there existed such an institution as a place at which murder passed unpunished, the best of us would become murderers. At least *I* should, but then I am a SNARLER."

The satiric usefulness of this viewpoint becomes clearer in Gilbert's account of the birthday celebration in France for Napoleon III. The Snarler begins by reporting his own embarrassment, expressing the thought that became the nucleus of "There Lived a King" in *The Gondoliers* over twenty years later: "Everybody turns out to be something municipal. I am distressed to find that the cobbler whom I bullied in such capital *patois* yesterday, is a deputy mayor, in blue and silver. . . . Everybody is somebody, except your Snarler, who (it would seem) is Nobody" ("Out-of-Town Talk," August 26, 1865, 141). This reminder of the Snarler's own bad British manners keeps the British reader from focusing entirely on the absurdities of the French, and the account of the high mass in the Emperor's honor contains more details to humble British pride: "I saw a curious, gaping crowd of brutal English, who chaffed the priests as they made collections, and for whom even the gigantic 'Suisse' had no terrors; and I saw a crowd of dirty, greasy Frenchmen and women, who went through the form of praying with about as much reverence as we English use when we say grace." The Snarler can say "we English" with satiric force, because he sees himself as a faulty and potentially criminal man.

As "Our Own Correspondent at a Murder Trial" (April 14, 1866, 43), the Snarler exploits his avowed deficiency in sympathy to stir the reader's compassion for a murderer and to arouse disgust with the frivolity of the spectators. The satire aims at shaming the vice of seeking a thrill in someone else's misfortune. The Snarler imitates insensitivity in his style, reporting the trial as if it were a social occasion: "Editor — In compliance with your request, I took the express last night to Turniptop, in order to be present at an Assize trial for murder. A more enjoyable day than that which I have just spent in the Turniptop Crown Court it has seldom been my lot to experience."

From this perverse viewpoint, the reporter focuses upon the audience, especially the "charming girls" with their expressions of "beaming expectancy." Seated with them in the gallery, he pretends to share their perspective. The murderer, seen through opera glasses, turns out to be a disappointment — "not much of a villain to look at, being small, dirty, and unwholesome in appearance." The report of the murder also disappoints the gallery. The man was charged with killing "his sweetheart (save the mark!) by kicking her on the head in the course of a drunken brawl." After the Snarler betrays his real viewpoint through his parenthesis, he again uses "we" as if he shared the young ladies' need for excitement. The report becomes a satire not only against the audience but against the school of "sensation" fiction — led by Mary Elizabeth Braddon and Wilkie Collins — which was often parodied by Gilbert, F. C. Burnand, and other writers for *Punch* and *Fun* during the 1860's:

> It was a common murder enough we (that is, the occupants of the gallery where the young ladies were, and I was) grieved to find. There was nothing sensational about it — there was no poisoning governess, with light hair and demon eyes; there was not a hint of a midnight attack on a solitary traveller in the midst of a wild heath; everything connected with the charge was filthy, coarse, and commonplace. So much the better, in one sense, for it entirely removed from the minds of the pretty girls in court any harrowing feeling of pity which a more refined or complicated murder would have aroused for the accused.

In widening the satire to include a broadside at sensational fiction, Gilbert aims at the same target that he often hits in his later works. It is not some flaw "out there" in one individual or institution; he is not pleading to end capital punishment or even to banish ladies from the galleries; for the target is within the minds of his audience. He attacks popular attitudes and the things that feed these attitudes, such as sensational novels. By focusing on the callousness of sentimental young ladies, he makes the public appetite for sensation stand out in bold relief, so that it can be seen and rejected as inhumane.

The details of the trial emphasize the callousness: the Snarler and the ladies "fidget" at the prospect of not hearing a death sentence; they grow bored with the witnesses and watch the young barristers, one of whom sketches a lady in the gallery, while another writes verses and still another makes a "cork man, with arms and legs of quill." As the cross-examination continues, "Newspapers are produced and circulated, and papers of sandwiches and flasks of sherry are handed to the young ladies, and the gallery where the young ladies are, and where I am, becomes the scene of a charming little improvised pic-nic." But, when the moment of real drama finally arrives, and the judge asks the jury for its verdict, the ladies rise and leave the courtroom, not daring to hear the long-awaited death sentence. That sensation is too much for the readers of *Lady Audley's Secret:*

A shriek in the crowd at the back of the court tells that the sentence has gone home somewhere, and then all is over.

Altogether the occupants of the gallery where the ladies were, and where I was, enjoyed themselves exceedingly.

SNARLER.

III   *The World Seen by "Bab"*

As satirical reporting, "Our Own Correspondent at a Murder Trial" ranks among Gilbert's best contributions to *Fun*. Anyone who reads the piece would surely be less inclined to view flippantly any criminal. But, so long as Gilbert wrote as a reporter, marked limits existed upon his inventiveness, no matter what persona he adopted. The Snarler, the Comic Physiognomist, the Correspondent Out for a Holiday, the art critic, and the theatrical reviewer were all writing as reporters; and what gives interest to some of their pieces is their point of view — their self-importance, or their ironic misanthropy, or their playfulness.

Gilbert moved, however, toward a more inventive role as a comic writer in the second half of the 1860's. Instead of merely reviewing plays, he was parodying them by 1866 in full-page spreads; at the end of that year, his first burlesque, *Dulcamara*, was produced at St. James' Theatre. His first full-length comedy, *An Old Score*, was produced in 1869; and his short stories were appearing in magazines and annuals. As his most important achievement of this decade, he began writing verses for *Fun* in so distinctive a style and tone that they became a unified series. In January, 1869, he gave them an inclusive title, The Bab Ballads; and, on February 6, he began numbering them, starting with number sixty.

His decision to start with that number was not whimsical. Roughly sixty verses previously, in the issue of June 1, 1867, "General John" had appeared, and with it the series began appearing regularly in *Fun*.[45] Until September, 1870, almost every other issue, and in some months every issue, contained a ballad illustrated by Gilbert. He included verses written before "General John" in published collections of *The Bab Ballads*, but few of them match the tone and style of the "Bab" who narrates the main series. Indeed, Bab is not even present in some of the early verse. In "To My Absent Husband," which appeared in *Punch* on October 14, 1865, (and was never reprinted by Gilbert), a nonsensical wife is the speaker:

> Tell me, Edward, dost remember
> How at breakfast often we,

> Put our bacon in the tea-pot
> While we took and fried our tea?[46]

The ending moves away from the echoes of Edward Lear and becomes mildly satirical: the couple allegedly "forgot" to pay for their goods, and the husband is absent because he is in prison. The whimsical humor perfected by Lear and Lewis Carroll did not lead Gilbert to any significant creations, except perhaps for "The Advent of Spring" in *Fun*, (February 1, 1862, 200) which remains an exuberant bit of nonsense.[47] But three of his better poems precede the main series of *The Bab Ballads*, and they are experiments in the use of a dramatized persona. "To the Terrestrial Globe" is a mock-Byronic soliloquy "by a Miserable Wretch" (September 30, 1865, 29); "The Pantomime 'Super' to His Mask" (February 24, 1866, 238), is a dialogue, since the mask is given the final word. The famous "Yarn of the Nancy Bell" (March 3, 1866, 242 - 43) is a framed narrative, like S. T. Coleridge's "The Rime of the Ancient Mariner," which it faintly parodies. In none of these early poems — unless in "The Yarn of the Nancy Bell" — does Bab appear with his amazing detachment while narrating outlandish events.

Though different in tone, the three works have strong thematic links with the regular *Bab Ballads*. They express Bab's vision of the world and his awareness of conflict as a principal element of society. The world, in "To the Terrestrial Globe," is marked by indifference: it "rolls on." Only Byronic egoism could allow a man to speak as if the universe would obey his commands: "Roll on, thou ball, roll on!" The futility of the command gives the speech its irony:

> It's true my butcher's bill is due;
> It's true my prospects all look blue —
> But don't let that unsettle you:
> Never *you* mind!
> Roll on!

The stage direction, "*[It rolls on.]*," followed by "Curtain" in the original version, puts a grim edge on the humor, enforcing the Byronic image of the earth's "pathless" course "Through seas of inky air." The theme of cosmic indifference is equally stressed in a later Bab ballad, which again makes fun of a Romantic attitude. "Sea-Side Snobs" (November 9, 1867, 88) is a parody of William Wordsworth's "Lines Written in Early Spring"; it is built upon the contrast between nature's cheerful unconcern and the speaker's disgust with the ill-bred young men at Margate:

> They buy unholy suits of clothes,
> And every day they don them;
> Their speech is crapulous with oaths,
> But still the sun shines on them!

Bab marvels that "Nature don't retire/ From public life disgusted."
His concluding realization nicely understates the theme of cosmic
indifference:

> Oh, sun and breeze and dancing trees,
> In one commingling blended,
> You are not difficult to please —
> Not easily offended.

Bab's sense of nature's unconcern leads to a deeper implication of
the theme: the suggestion that no providential force cares for the
right or wrong of human actions. Passages in Gilbert's writing at this
period suggest that he wanted to challenge the convention of poetic
justice in popular fiction and melodrama. He entitled one of his
short stories "The Triumph of Vice" (1867), and he ended the
original version with a sardonic though ambiguous "Moral," printed
in Gothic type: "Thus, notwithstanding all that has been said to the
contrary, vice is sometimes triumphant. Cunning, malice, and im-
posture may not flourish directly they are practiced, but depend
upon it, my dear children, that they will assert their own in the
end."[48]

This view was a direct affront to the moralistic tradition, and it oc-
cured just after Lewis Carroll had made Alice forget in Wonderland
all the lessons from Isaac Watts. Gilbert's scorn for the tradition was
focused on the "sensation drama," the object of his burlesque in *Fun*
titled "Vice Triumphant" (November 11, 1865, 88 - 89). The fictitious author, an "Aged Curate," complains that sensational dramas
are untrue to nature in introducing vice simply for it to be
overwhelmed in the last act: "I, for one, have spent a long and
laborious life in the exercise of the strictest virtue, and I have never
triumphed."

In the cosmos seen by Bab, anything can happen. Murder can go
unpunished, as it does in "Gentle Alice Brown"; or an honest man,
in "The Folly of Brown," can resist and infuriate a dishonest stock
jobber. In "The Three Bohemian Ones," the reckless boys inherit
the fortune which their father had meant to give to a hospital: vice

triumphs "by dint of accident" (April 10, 1869, 51). Bab comforts the moralistic reader with a rationalization that only strengthens the idea that success and virtue have no inherent connection:

> By strange exceptions Virtue deigns
> To prove how paramount she reigns;
> A standing rule I do not know
> That's been more oft established so.

Romantic convention may delude people into believing that fate will be providential: in "Little Oliver," the page boy imagines that an earl's daughter will marry him, simply because she sings songs about high-born ladies who fell in love with their servants. But the earl squelches the boy's hopes, and Bab contrasts Romantic convention with his own sense of reality.

> Now I'm prepared to bet a guinea,
> Were this a mere dramatic case,
> The page would have eloped with MINNIE,
> But, no — he only left his place.
>
> The simple Truth is my detective,
> With me Sensation can't abide;
> The Likely beats the mere Effective,
> And Nature is my only guide.
> (December 5, 1868, 132)

In an "unjust world" in which virtue triumphs "only in theatrical performances,"[49] everyone is on his own; and the basic task is survival. The lone survivor of the good ship "Nancy Bell" chants his "single joke" in melancholy triumph. His is a story of how the struggle to live dwarfs every other concern, of how the most rigid taboos vanish when one person thinks that his identity can only be preserved at the expense of another's:

> "Then only the cook and me was left,
> And the delicate question, 'Which
> Of us two goes to the butcher?' arose,
> And we argued it out as sich."

Neither man questions the priority of survival over love and friendship:

> "For I loved the cook as a brother, I did,
>   And the cook he worshipped me;
> But we'd both be blowed if we'd either be stowed
>   In the other chap's hold, you see."

The cannibalism which disgusted the editors of *Punch* illustrates the common Victorian theme of social competition; and the struggle for personal advancement leads toward this brutal image. The world of Dickens' *Great Expectations* (1861) is filled with persons such as Miss Havisham, Pumblechook, and Magwich, who use other people for their own ends, and the child growing up in this world is plagued with fears of being eaten. "Your heart and your liver shall be tore out, roasted and ate," Magwich tells Pip in the first chapter, and the adults at the Christmas dinner trouble the boy by speculating on the sort of main dish he would have made, had he been born a pig. Of all images of human exploitation, cannibalism is the most explicit, there being no more literal way to treat a person as an object than by eating him.

Competition was one fact of Victorian life which made the image appropriate, even before Charles Darwin's theory gave this activity deeper significance. The mere introduction of competitive examinations in a government office horrifies one of Trollope's characters whose vision domesticates the appalling image of humanity as "monsters of the deep" who prey on one another in *King Lear* (IV, ii): " 'The world,' said Mrs. Woodward, 'will soon be like a fish pond, very full of fish, but with very little food for them. Every one is scrambling for the other's prey, and they will end at last by eating one another.' "[50] In "The Yarn of the Nancy Bell," Gilbert treats literally what other writers used as a metaphor to express their fears for a society endangered by status-seeking.

Competition is the normal human relationship in *The Bab Ballads*, and many of the characters seem to accept wholeheartedly the dictum of the Comic Physiognomist:

Man was sent into the world to contend with man, and to get the advantage of him in every possible way. Whenever the C. P. happens to see a human being in the act of assisting, directly or indirectly, another human being, he pictures to himself a foot-race in which the candidates are constantly giving place to each other from motives of sheer politeness. The great object of life is to be first at the winning-post, and so that a man attains that end, and yet goes conscientiously over the whole course, it matters nothing how many of his fellow candidates he hustles on the way. ("Concerning Some Bald People," March 9, 1867, 261)

A few of Gilbert's characters do give place to others out of sheer politeness. General John apparently has no other reason for trading ranks with Private James. By the exchange, he atones for his first response — an "aristocratical sneer" — when James asked him to trade places, and he escapes the private's reproach:

> "No truly great or generous cove
>   Deserving of them names,
> Would sneer at a fixed idea that's drove
>   In the mind of a PRIVATE JAMES!"

From the "C. P.'s" viewpoint, Captain Reece would be another polite fool who neglects his own interests by catering to his crewmen, letting them marry his female relatives (who were engaged to peers), and consenting, on his part, to marry the Boatswain's mother. But the normal, assertive response is Captain Joyce's in "Joe Golightly; or, The First Lord's Daughter" (October 12, 1867, 54). Rather than allow a common sailor to marry his child, he sentences Joe to "Twelve years' black hole," with daily floggings.

By focusing upon the struggle for social advancement, Gilbert may have been glancing at the agitation over the Reform Bill of 1867. The proposal to extend the franchise to some of the working classes had been hotly debated during 1866 and the first half of 1867, but the Bill finally passed in August. What the Tory prime minister, Lord Derby, called a "leap in the dark"[51] remained an object of controversy. In "Shooting Niagara: And After?" Thomas Carlyle imagined the direst consequences, including "mutinous maidservants"; and he compared the aristocrats who supported the Bill to an Irish carpenter who showed his talents by sawing off the plank he was sitting on.[52] The Comic Physiognomist might have said that they were giving place to others in the foot-race of life.

"General John" appeared soon after two events which would have heightened Gilbert's awareness of the class struggle: in May, 1867, a massive demonstration for reform had been held at Hyde Park in defiance of the Home Secretary; and in the previous month Gilbert's friend, T. W. Robertson, produced his new comedy, *Caste*, which dealt with "that often discussed question of political economy — unequal matches" (*Fun*, April 20, 1867. 63). The play echoed the theme of Gilbert's poem, "Only a Dancing Girl" (June 23, 1866, 146), a portrait of a low-born woman whose virtue makes her worthy of a place among the respectable ladies who scorn her profession. But Robertson's play was far from recommending the total abolition of caste. To the relief of *The Times*, the heroine's drunken father appeared as a caricature of the Radicals, and from his mouth came "that democratic claptrap which is among the leading nuisances of the day" (April 11, 1867, 11). Since this derelict was contrasted with an industrious comic gasman who accepted the caste system, the play implied that only the dregs of society would welcome indiscriminate leveling.

This sort of leveling occurs on board that strange ship *The Mantelpiece* in Gilbert's ballad, "Captain Reece," published in *Fun* on February 8, 1868. In it, the lower classes are a crew of cunning opportunists whose representative, posing as a "nervous, shy, low-spoken man," dares to suggest that the captain's relatives marry the sailors:

> "If you'd ameliorate our life,
> Let each select from them a wife;
> And as for nervous me, old pal,
> Give me your own enchanting gal!"

In the sequel, "The Martinet" (February 13, 1869, 228), the same sailor strikes at the new captain for refusing to shake hands. The crew of the "saucy *Mantelpiece*" eventually shoots this disciplinarian, and the Admiralty restores the permissive Reece to his command. If these fantasies reflected public anxiety over reform, Gilbert left their implications to the whimsy or prejudice of his readers. Did he imply that permissiveness was the lesser of evils, now that the workers demanded a political voice, or was he suggesting Carlyle's view that exploitation of the rich by the poor would be the price of democracy? Reece assists in his own social leveling by pampering his crewmen; from the middle-class viewpoint of a Bounderby, he whets the poor man's appetite for turtle soup and venison.

But a deeper satiric target is Reece's obsession with duty — his sense that he must stop at nothing to make his crew happy. This conviction illustrates in extreme form two ethical doctrines that were controversial in the 1860's. One was the Utilitarian injunction to create the greatest good for the greatest number; the other — more unsettling because more specific — was John Ruskin's application of the Golden Rule to political economy. In the first of Ruskin's notorious essays for the *Cornhill Magazine* (August, 1860), he proclaimed that the manufacturer had a "paternal" responsibility for his workers; and two of his illustrations foreshadow the exemplary conduct of Captain Reece. Manufacturers should be like military leaders, Ruskin felt, for "the officer who has the most direct personal relations with his men, the most care for their interests . . . will develop their effective strength, through their affection for his own person, and trust in his character, to a degree wholly unattainable by other means."[53] Just such an officer, Reece is "adored by all his men," and he behaves like the ideal captain in Ruskin's final illustration:

Supposing the captain of a frigate saw it right, or were by chance obliged, to place his own son in the position of a common sailor: as he would then treat his son, he is bound always to treat every one of the men under him. . . .

And as the captain of a ship is bound to be the last man to leave his ship in case of wreck, and to share his last crust with the sailors in case of famine, so the manufacturer, in any commercial crisis or distress, is bound to take the suffering of it with his men, and even to take more of it for himself than he allows his men to feel; as a father would in a famine, or battle, sacrifice himself for his son.[54]

Reece follows this "only effective, true, or practical RULE" to its logical end; but what appears noble in adversity may seem absurd in prosperity. His self-sacrifice consists of supplying his crew with *Saturday Reviews*, featherbeds, valets, ices, and wealthy brides. That his altruism is completely unbelievable enforces the ridicule of an ideal which Bab, without voicing the slightest criticism, clearly presents as unrealistic, given the selfish nature of men. The poem may read more like nonsense than satire, but the improbability of it creates the satiric point: for a man to act with complete altruism, merely from an obsession with duty, is absurd. Ruskin's own teachings had been called "absolute nonsense"[55] (and he himself labeled "crazy and ignorant");[56] for Gilbert to create a fantastic character who acts upon Ruskin's principles was perhaps a more civil way of criticizing his position. Yet Reece's foolishness is impressive: he has a touch of Don Quixote's comic sanctity, and he stays uncontaminated by the "self-help" morality of a competitive world.

Unlike Reece, however, most of Bab's characters fight back. The plots of the ballads bristle with keen rivalries; sexual rivalry in particular accounts for much of their brutality. In "Ellen McJones Aberdeen" (March 21, 1868, 16), the Scots piper is sliced in half by his English rival; a jealous sultan drowns an English officer in "The Scornful Colonel" (September 25, 1869, 31); jealous mermen amputate the Captain's well-shaped legs in "The Captain and the Mermaids" (November 7, 1868, 85); the prototype of Wilfred Shadbolt tries to behead his rival in "Annie Protheroe" (October 24, 1868, 65). Moreover, professional rivalries are equally violent. Bloody retaliation is threatened against Hopley Porter for his mildness in "The Rival Curates"; and "Damon v. Pythias" (March 26, 1870, 31) ends with the two competing counsels pushing each other off a cliff. Even the supernatural realm (at least in the theater) is competitive in "The Ghost, the Gallant, the Gael, and the Goblin," (March 14, 1868, 6): "Which of us two is Number One — /The ghostie, or the goblin?" The continual asking of such questions underlies the restlessness and conflict of Bab's world.

At its most intense, the sense of rivalry pervades "The Baby's Vengeance" (January 16, 1869, 188) in which fantasy blends with psychological realism to expose the roots of this feeling. The poem, which has an unusually complex structure for a Bab ballad, begins with the customary narrative quatrains as Bab reports the misery of Paley Vollaire, the ruined son of wealthy parents:

> Shabby and sorry and sorely sick,
> He slept, and dreamt that the clock's "tick, tick,"
> Was one of the Fates, with a long sharp knife,
> Snicking off bits of his shortened life.

Then Vollaire becomes the speaker, telling Frederick West of his miserable infancy; the stanzas lengthen to six lines, and the rhymes change, enforcing the sense of a person making an intimate disclosure. Vollaire reveals that his real mother was a wet nurse who neglected her son, and he paints as vivid a picture of infant jealousy as St. Augustine's in *The Confessions*. Vollaire's sense of betrayal seems to rekindle as he reports it:

> "Two little babes dwelt in her humble cot:
>   One was her own — the other only lent to her:
> *Her own she slighted.* Tempted by a lot
>   Of gold and silver regularly sent to her,
> She ministered unto the little other
> In the capacity of foster-mother.
>
> *I was her own.* Oh, how I lay and sobbed
>   In my poor cradle — deeply, deeply cursing
> The rich man's pampered bantling, who had robbed
>   My only birthright — an attentive nursing!"

Bab's drawing shows the indignant baby putting the intruder into his own cradle so he can trade places, but the comic impossibilities do not conceal the sense of genuine resentment and injury. Vollaire's feeling is perfectly expressed when he calls his rival "the little other." His loss of an "attentive nursing" means the loss of love; the image relates to other instances in Gilbert's work where eating represents the fullest gratification.

> So great a luxury was food, I think
>   No wickedness but I was game to try for it.
> *Now* if I wanted anything to drink
>   At any time, I only had to cry for it!
> *Once,* if I dared to weep, the bottle lacking,
> My blubbering involved a serious smacking!

But trading places does not assuage Vollaire's resentment against the world. As an adult, he squanders all his falsely inherited wealth; apparently he lives without love for any creature. His confession turns out to be a second means of taking vengeance on Frederick West; for, trading places once more, Vollaire assumes West's savings,

> And FRED (entitled to all things there)
> He took the fever from MR. VOLLAIRE,
> Which killed poor FREDERICK WEST. Meanwhile
> VOLLAIRE sailed off to Madeira's isle.

Through cunning, and West's gullibility, and the fantastic workings of Bab's universe, Vollaire wins twice in the footrace of life.

When survival or an attractive prize is not the goal, conflicts in the ballads arise from the struggle to preserve one's social identity — one's chosen persona. In "The Rival Curates," a man's image is at stake: the Reverend Clayton Hooper insists upon being known as "the mildest curate going." He therefore prepares to assassinate the Reverend Hopley Porter. Bloodshed becomes unnecessary, however, because Porter is weary of his own clerical mildness:

> "What?" said that reverend gent,
>   "Dance through my hours of leisure?
> Smoke? — bathe myself with scent? —
>   Play croquêt? Oh, with pleasure!"

Questions of identity arise throughout Gilbert's work — the plots involving swapped infants show how literally he could treat the question of "Who am I?" The issue becomes most complex when it concerns the relationship of a person to his role. "The Rival Curates" illustrates opposite forms of this relationship: fantastic commitment to maintaining a persona, on the one hand, and eagerness to escape from it on the other.

The eagerness to escape is the subject of the pre-Bab verse, "The Pantomime 'Super' to his Mask," which was one of Gilbert's favorites,[57] perhaps because it so directly expressed a central concern. The speaker is an actor in rebellion against a literal persona, the mask which he has worn at the pantomime; for the mask is the "Beast that destroys't my heaven-born identity!" But "*The Mask respondeth,*" and its questions imply that the actor is as far as ever from realizing his true being:

> Oh! master mine,
> Look thou within thee, ere again ill-using me.
> Art thou aware
> Of nothing there
> Which might abuse thee, as thou art abusing me?
> A brain that mourns at *thine* unredeemed rascality?
> A soul that weeps at *thy* threadbare morality?
> Both grieving that *their* individuality
> Is merged in thine?

The actor is invited to see himself from the inside out, and what he sees are layers of masks that distort his humanity as much as the one he has just taken off. The implications of this vision move Gilbert toward a serious portrayal of experience; the tone is sober here, despite the burlesque of theatrical rhetoric. In other poems such as "Only a Dancing Girl" and "Disillusioned," the contrast between the public image and the inner self leads Gilbert to write with unusual seriousness. For him, the compulsion to wear a mask makes people comic; the urge to take it off and live freely raises such difficulties that the strugglers for liberation have to be taken seriously.

Comedy dominates the ballads because they focus on "the present artificial state of society" in which wearing masks is a major enterprise. The clergy are among the most adept of Gilbert's characters at sustaining artifice. The Reverend Simon Magus conceals his worldliness in pious rhetoric as he rationalizes about buying a living in a parish of noble families: "I might show these men of birth/The hollowness of rank on earth"; and he neatly justifies simony when he learns who is making the sale:

> "A Jew?" said SIMON, "happy find!
> I purchase this advowson, mind.
> My life shall be devoted to
> Converting that unhappy Jew!"
> ("The Reverend Simon Magus," February 5, 1870, 215.)

Conversion, for Gilbert's clergymen, means changing masks; the Jewish busman who finally yields to a relentless bishop acquires Anglo-Saxon features, fair whiskers, and a place in society ("The Bishop and the Busman," August 17, 1867, 242). A still more aggressive mask-changer is the colonial bishop who creates an artificial society among the innocent natives of Canoodle-Dum. Talking with their "Chum, or High Priest,"

> He found that at sunrise they were summoned to prayer by the beating of a tom-tom, or the blowing of a horn.
> "It does not matter which," said the Chum.
> "How is this?" said the Bishop. "It does not matter which?"
> "It does not the least matter, whether it is a tom-tom or a horn," said the Chum. "Why should it?"
> "Oh," said the Bishop. "This is a terrible state of things." And he thought to himself, "It is useless, just at present, to endeavour to inculcate the beauties of Christianity." ("A Christian Frame of Mind," January 8, 1870, 175)

Against the demand for ritual in society, for rigid definitions of proper and improper conduct, one of Bab's characters emerges as a hero. This is "lost Mr. Blake," who would never have accepted the Bishop's argument that the mold of a plum pudding matters more than the ingredients. Bab himself acts scandalized at "Belial" Blake, "that outcast of society," who

> used to say that he would no more think of interfering
> with his priest's robes than with his church or his steeple,
> And that he did not consider his soul imperilled because
> somebody over whom he had no influence whatever,
> chose to dress himself up like an ecclesiastical GUY FAWKES.
> ("Lost Mr. Blake," November 28, 1868, 121:
> this text follows Gilbert's revision.)

In long lines imitating the effect of liturgical chanting, Bab tells how Mr. Blake cured his wife's passion for churchgoing by dragging her to twelve different services on Sundays and by forcing her to put her

housekeeping money in the collection plate. After doing her servants' chores on the Sabbath, "She soon began to find that even
charity, if you allow it to interfere with your personal luxuries,
becomes an intolerable bore." Now her evenings are spent with Mr.
Blake in "connubial fondlings," though the indignant narrator
wonders "where in the world (or rather, out of it) they expect to go!"

In satirizing the return of ritualism to the Anglican Church,
Gilbert expressed his general sense of how arbitrary social decorum
can become. Sheer arbitrariness is the only explanation for a
prelate's sudden refusal to learn a certain dance step in "The Bishop
of Rum-ti-Foo" (November 16, 1867, 104). This clergyman, who has
done so many unconventional things by English standards (he has
eaten scalps soaked in rum to please the natives), learns a series of
grotesque routines from a street dancer, but abruptly draws the line
at holding his ankle while hopping:

> "No," said the worthy Bishop, "No;"
> That is a length to which, I trow,
> Colonial Bishops cannot go."

Arbitrariness typifies Gilbert's vision of social taboos and values.
Ritualism is not confined to Anglican clerics: the middle classes are
eager to worship through their own secular rituals any person of rank
or wealth. The public bows to the valet of the Prince Il Baleine (the
Prince of "Whale[s]");[58] their interest in royalty turns into fetishism:

> "And this then is the hand
> That combs at his command?
> Oh, please, do let me kiss it!"
> ("Prince Il Baleine," August 28, 1869, 253.)

The crowd's "joy insane" in kotowing to his valet helps to perpetrate
an artificial society, one based on arbitrary rather than real values.

Perhaps the culmination of this theme and of Gilbert's artistry in
The Bab Ballads is "Etiquette," first published in the Christmas
number of *Graphic* on December 25, 1869 (6 - 7). Bondage to the
"arbitrary rule of etiquette" causes the problems of two polite
Englishmen who are shipwrecked on an island without being
properly introduced. Each dwells in isolation: Peter Gray on the
northern half, among the oysters, which he detests; Somers, who
lives among the turtles on the southern half of the island, longs for

oysters. The artificial state of their society gives way to nature when, on overhearing a soliloquy, Peter discovers that they have known a mutual friend and may therefore speak to each other. Friendship blossoms; and each gorges on his favorite food until a shipload of convicts arrives with their mutual friend on board. Now the two men snub each other for knowing so disreputable a person; they "cut each other dead," and the repressive society exists once more:

> To allocate the island they agreed by word of mouth,
> And PETER takes the north again, and SOMERS takes the south.
> And PETER has the oysters, which he hates, in layers thick,
> And SOMERS has the turtle — turtle always makes him sick.

This ballad illustrates the qualities of Gilbert's best satiric verse. As a secular parable, it tells a simple story with an important theme; and it makes snobbery appear all the more absurd by showing its effects upon a society of two. The imagery focuses on one object, the food that represents what Gray and Somers lose by maintaining their sense of propriety. As narrator, Bab achieves the relationship with his readers that makes him a memorable, if elusive, persona. The greatest absurdity in the poem is his calm way of reporting grotesque behavior as if nothing could be more natural. He passes no judgment upon the two Englishmen, leaving that to the reader.

Bab's unruffled concern with details distinguishes him from the Comic Physiognomist and the ever-complaining Snarler. He is stating a fact, not voicing a criticism, when he reports Gray's feelings: "The oysters at his feet aside impatiently he shoved,/For turtle and his mother were the only things he loved." At the outset, when Bab does sound moralistic, a line of heavy bathos reveals a mind with a bewildering notion of his reader's responses:

> The *Ballyshannon* foundered off the coast of Cariboo,
> And down in fathoms many went the captain and the crew;
> Down went the owners — greedy men whom hope of gain allured:
> Oh, dry the starting tear, for they were heavily insured.

This dead-pan tone and the concreteness of Bab's reporting make "Etiquette" one of Gilbert's finest satires of social inhibition. In a letter to Dante Gabriel Rossetti, Algernon Swinburne called it a "splendid 'Bab' ": "I thought it one of the best — and it took me almost an hour to read it out en famille owing to the incessant explosions and collapses of reader and audience in tears and roars of laughter."[59] Today, we may not respond so boisterously; but, knowing how Swinburne's own verse in the 1860's so offended Victorian proprieties, we can understand his delight in Gilbert's straight-faced ridicule of repressed behavior.

After reading the ballads in the context of Gilbert's other journalism, we may also begin to understand why G. K. Chesterton ranked them above the Savoy operas.[60] They convey a bold vision of men's pretenses at having attained order in an unstable world. They expose characters in the act of maintaining this illusion through clinging to a persona, as Simon Magus does in playing the role of a pious clergyman. They show how obsessively people rely upon systems — rituals, laws, rules of ethics and etiquette — to give life the semblance of order, and thereby neglect the possibility of living freely, even happily, as the two marooned Englishmen lived before being trapped once more by their sense of propriety.

Gilbert's darker poems provide a significant background for the themes of the humorous ones. "At a Pantomime" reads almost like a song of experience, bringing into Bab's world an awareness of facts that loom above the trivial concerns of his comic figures. Though the children at the pantomime "clap and crow," the elders see Father Christmas as a skeleton:

> The old ones, palsied, blear, and hoar,
> Their breasts in anguish beat —
> They've seen him seventy times before,
> How well they know that cheat!
> (December 28, 1867, 165)

Knowing "Starvation, — Poor Law Union Fare," "cold and want and death," "They wearily sit, and grimly long/For the Transformation Scene." Against this serious background, Bab's characters appear all the more absurd by treating etiquette, royalty, or social status as if it were the crucial fact of their existence. Death by itself dwarfs the concerns of an artificial society.

The ballads are also bold in entertaining a view of reality that offers no simplistic sense of providence, no consistent poetic justice, and no assurance of the rightness of one's goals and values. Bab dared to dream of Tospy-Turveydom where "vice is virtue — virtue vice" ("My Dream," March 19, 1870, 15), and to suggest to those Victorians who put their faith in moral absolutes that this world might be one of moral relativism. Against the vision of the terrestrial globe rolling on its "pathless" course, Bab shows how men persist in investing objects and rules with absolute value and absolute authority. Between the little circles of their awareness and the vast, ignored stage on which they act, such incongruity exists that Bab can offer a comic vision of human rivalries, codes, and ambitions. The vision becomes satiric as well as comic whenever Bab helps us to remember alternatives: Captain Reece does not have to be a slave of duty; Somers and Gray do not have to deprive themselves of companionship and their favorite foods. But in Bab's world, to be natural "is always unbusiness-like," and his comic figures cling to their obsessions unless freedom comes to them, as it did for Hopley Porter, in the only way they can respect — by "compulsion."

CHAPTER 2

Exploring Two Worlds:
Gilbert as Playwright

GILBERT's pursuit of the mind into its fantasies involved a continual examination of two themes, "the melodrama and the fairy-tales of his epoch."[1] This interest led him into the Victorian theater where melodrama fed the dream of virtue amply rewarded, and where pantomime dissolved reality in spectacular transformation scenes, only to order it again in the stylized fun of the Harlequinade. The stage had attracted Gilbert since his youth: he reportedly wrote fifteen farces and burlesques by the time he was twenty-four;[2] he seemed bound, sooner or later, to become a dramatist.

But the spell of the theater had weakened by the time his first plays were produced, if his poem, "Disillusioned — by an Ex-enthusiast," is true to his experience. Here the stage becomes a metaphor of lost illusions, while an adult complains of no longer seeing the glory of his old heroes:

> Would that ye always shone, who write,
> Bathed in your own innate limelight,
>   And ye who battle wage,
> Or that in darkness I had died
> Before my soul had ever sighed
>   To see you off the stage![3]

The same discrepancy between romantic illusion and everyday reality gives a double existence to Gilbert's heroine in *Princess Toto* (1876):

> I have two worlds — I live two lives —
>   One here, and one elsewhere;
> In each of them men marry wives,
>   And love them here and there.

This world that rolls about the sun
With sin and sorrow teems;
The other, and the fairer one
Is called the world of dreams.[4]

From his own childhood — "the most miserable period of our existence"[5] — Gilbert learned that the theater could compensate for the disappointments of day-to-day living. Visits to the pantomime were "absolute realizations of a fairy mythology which I had almost incorporated with my religious faith." In those innocent times before he had "any idea of a Harlequin who spent the day hours in a pair of trousers and a bad hat," he imagined that to become Harlequin or Columbine would be the height of a man or a woman's happiness, but being Pantaloon and Clown seemed a "fitting purgatory" for a life misspent. But with age Gilbert began to prefer Clown; and, when he returned to the theater as a dramatist, he explored its world from something close to Clown's mischievous point of view.

I *Beginnings: Understanding Pantomime*

What dreams could Victorians realize through the pantomime and melodrama? What made the pantomime so exciting that as the curtain rose one heard "a great gasping a-ha-a from a thousand children's throats"?[6] Thackeray's report of an imaginary performance outlines the framework of its appeal. The first of the two main sections of a pantomime — the opening or the introduction — represents the trials of a hero and heroine who normally come from some popular myth or fairy tale.[7] A good fairy takes the hero's side against the pantomime monarch — the heroine's father in Thackeray's skit — and, just as the hero faces death, she descends like a goddess from a machine: "the Fairy Bandanna . . . in her amaranthine car drawn by Paphian doves, appeared and put a stop to the massacre."[8] Her magic creates the Transformation Scene, when the lovers become Harlequin and Columbine, the pantomime monarch becomes Pantaloon, and his two giants become the first and the second Clown. The rest of the piece is the Harlequinade, dominated by Clown's slapstick buffoonery and violent practical joking.

In both sections, the audience could predict what would happen. The hero would fall into danger, face death, and be rescued; the Transformation Scene would open splendid vistas at the back of the stage; the Harlequinade would teem with familiar comic business: "When a young lady appears at the wing in a fashionable fur tippet, every child knows that that fashionable fur tippet will be stolen by clown before she reaches the opposite wing, and that she will walk off abstractedly without missing it. When a tinker appears on the stage we all know that clown is going to burn Society with that tinker's hot iron" ("The Physiognomist at the Play," *Fun*, January 16, 1864, 181). By the time the pantomime ended, it would have offered two different stimulants for juvenile fantasies. One would be romantic adventure, enriched with music, dance, and elaborate scenery; the other would be farcical mischief in a world where policemen can be tripped and where babies are smashed with no moral consequences.

Gilbert's critical outlook made him discontented with the moral neutrality of the pantomime. He was too much of a satirist to welcome the rowdy Harlequinade as the "quintessence of comedy"; unlike Charles Baudelaire, who returned elated from a performance of an English pantomime, Gilbert could not abandon himself to an "intoxication of laughter" over Clown's antics — "something both terrible and irresistible."[9] Gilbert called it a "vacant and un-reasonable enjoyment" (*Fun*, January 16, 1864, 181), and in verse fantasy he explored the significance of the Harlequinade's amoral appeal. "The Story of Gentle Archibald" suggests that its appeal comes from the acting out of aggressive impulses (May 19, 1866, 100 - 101). A visit to the theater destroys the "gentle nature" of a child noted for "mild, respectful fun." Archibald immediately decides that his goal in life is to become Clown, much to the distress of his father, who has destined him for the church. But the boy achieves in dreams what his father denies: and, as Clown, he terrorizes the household, singling out every person in authority for special harrass-ment. After thrashing his nurse, boiling his little sister, and painting his "aged mother blue," he

> Put pussy in his father's soup;
> Placed beetles in his uncle's shoe;
> Cut a policeman right in two;
> Spread devastation round — and, ah,
> He red-hot-pokered his papa!

But complete wish-fulfillment is more than the boy can stand. The dream seems far more real than Clown's pranks in the theater; and, when the boy's conscience awakens, he begs the good fairy to

transform him back into his gentle self. As an examination of the
mind in pursuit of fantasy, the poem shows how the Harlequinade
appeals to repressed aggressions, which perhaps explains some of
Gilbert's discomfort when sitting among a pantomime audience,
where the laughter must have been a "release from constraint" at
the violation of social laws.[10] For persons who possessed "too much
justice and good sense — / To laugh at other folks' expense," the
fantasy could be delightful only when kept at a distance in the
theater; but total involvement with Clown's role sends Archibald
running back to reality.

As a critic, Gilbert suggested changing the pantomime in ways
that would appeal to the good sense of the audience; and his
proposed reforms are at once moral and esthetic. Signing himself
"Unity is Strength," he argues for greater coherence between the
opening and the Harlequinade. In an ideal pantomime, the plot of
the opening would be developed by Harlequin, Columbine, Pantaloon, and Clown, whose costumes should remind the audience of
their counterparts in the initial plot.[11] The roles of Harlequin and
Columbine would become rewards for virtue; that of Pantaloon, the
punishment for the autocratic pantomime monarch; and Gilbert's
Clown would have to play his tricks with a genuine fear of retribu-
tion.

In "A Consistent Pantomime," published two months before the
first night of *Trial by Jury* (1875), Gilbert suggests that Clown's
lawless career should lead straight to the courtroom where slapstick
would give way to satire. Clown's terror of the law, "mingling with
his keen sense of the absurdity of entrusting a man's fate to the decision of twelve men picked from the most ignorant, narrow-minded,
opinionated, intolerant and dishonest class of civilised beings in
London, will afford a clown-actor another opportunity of rescuing
his *rôle* from the contempt into which he has fallen."[12] Harlequin's
magic would advance the satire "by causing annoying placards to
appear on the walls, such as 'This gentleman was raised to the Bench
for Voting with his Party,' or by hanging inscriptions on the necks of
the jury, describing the various adulterations they habitually introduce into the wares in which they deal." Gilbert's courtroom and
placards would transform the Harlequinade into a vision of two
worlds — one magical and one real, filled with the ironies of life in
London. Instead of escape and "unreasonable enjoyment," his
reformed pantomime would offer a critical picture of how things
are.[13]

None of Gilbert's dramatic criticism is purely theoretical, and his remarks about the pantomime show his practical concern not only to understand but to improve a staple form of entertainment. He could not afford to ignore the form which gave most of his audience their first experience of the theater, for what had delighted people in childhood was bound to affect their expectations and demands as adults. The influence of the pantomime was also reflected in the resources of a theatrical company in which the beginning playwright would discover that the four principal actors were rough counterparts of Clown, Pantaloon, Harlequin, and Columbine. A company would contain a principal comedian, a "heavy" father, and a man and a woman for the romantic leads.[14] Because of this nucleus of actors and because remembered pantomimes were in virtually everyone's mind, new domestic comedies or melodramas might reveal the outlines of the more primitive genre: *Punch* cruelly discerned the four principals of the Harlequinade in Gilbert's unsuccessful melodrama, *Brantinghame Hall* (1888).[15] A Victorian dramatist needed to know the pantomime in order to understand both his materials and his audience. Consciously or not, he was apt to show its influence.

Gilbert was more fascinated by the pattern of transformation than by the opportunity to work within the genre. Though he wrote more than one pantomime in the 1860's, not until 1904 in *The Fairy's Dilemma, An Original Domestic Pantomime*, did he directly illustrate what he had meant by uniting the Harlequinade with the plot of the opening. In this play, the characters retain marks of their identity after being transformed: as Harlequin, a young clergyman keeps his spectacles and feels embarrassed in his new costume; the Judge, on becoming Pantaloon, says, "Deary me! it's not as great a change as I should have supposed!"[16] Mortified by their own antics in the Harlequinade, the characters demand a second transformation, a return to real life. Fantasy becomes as unbearable for them as it did for the boy who dreamed of being Clown.

Their experience points toward many of Gilbert's dramas in which transformation is a central motif. In a stark form of the motif, the "lozenge plot" of *The Mountebanks* (1892) haunted him — and Sullivan — for almost a decade: the opera's first act ends as transformation begins, with everyone becoming what they pretend to be. Other magical transformations occur in *Creatures of Impulse* (1871); in *The Sorcerer* (1877); and, most successfully, in *Iolanthe* (1882) — first when the Fairy Queen gives Strephon political invulnerability, making him a parliamentary Harlequin, and at the end when the peers are transformed into peri.

Without conventional magic, the many reversals and exchanges of roles — as in "General John" — are another expression of this motif. Ralph Rackstraw steps into the captain's uniform through the power of Buttercup's barely credible revelation; Grosvenor becomes commonplace at the threat of a "nephew's curse." In mass transformations of this sort, actors take over Mount Olympus in *Thespis* (1871) and a royal court in *The Grand Duke* (1896). A deeper kind of transformation results from magic in *The Palace of Truth* (1870), when the characters lose their ability to lie.

Each of these changes reflects in some degree the central action of the pantomime; but Gilbert usually adds another movement to the basic pattern: the return from fantasy to the limitations of the real world. The return is a second transformation, providing a dénouement, as at the end of *The Fairy's Dilemma*. It brings everyone out of the Palace of Truth, returns the Grand Duke to his throne, the gods to Olympus; it changes the monks back into bandits in *The Mountebanks*; it breaks the spell in *The Sorcerer* and *Creatures of Impulse*; it turns Galatea back into stone. Reality intrudes, waking everyone from his pantomime dream.

II   *Criticizing Victorian Drama: The Parody Reviews*

Gilbert's concern with theatrical convention and illusion is also expressed in his early reviews, parodies, and operatic burlesques. In demanding that pantomimes have unity — "dramatic interest, probability, and natural sequence of events"[17] — he was thinking not only of how to hold the attention of the audience but also of how to offer an entertainment, which, no matter how fantastic, appealed to reason. His commitment to "probability" sounds surprising until he clarifies his position. Probability, he suggests, is of two kinds: "social probability," which describes the actions of characters who behave as conventional people might in real life, and esthetic probability, which is exemplified by characters who behave according to the conventions of a particular genre of literature.

Gilbert explained the distinction in reviewing a farce, where "nothing appears so probable as that a policeman in a tablecloth should be mistaken for an apparition, except, perhaps, that when an honest and otherwise respectable gentleman loses his clothes at a hotel he should break open the first portmanteau he comes across, and dress himself up in the jockey-clothes of its proprietor. But these 'situations,' obtained though they be at the expense of social probability, are always amusing. . . ."[18] With this Aristotelian sense of probable improbabilities, Gilbert was well on the way in 1865 toward achieving the insight that led to the inner logic of his "fairy comedies" and fantastically conceived libretti.

In serious drama, however, he was less tolerant of departures from "social probability," though the illusion of a coherent world on the stage could temper his criticism. While other reviewers ridiculed Dion Boucicault's ignorance of university life and of Latin in *Formosa*, Gilbert ended his one-page parody with either an admission of Boucicault's artistry or a slap at the audience. He called the plot "very absurd and impossible . . . from a common-sense point of view, but very effective in a dramatic sense" (*Fun*, August 28, 1869, 255). From a dramatist's practical viewpoint, being "effective" is what counts. But normally for Gilbert, "the Likely beats the mere Effective," and "artistic verisimilitude" — Pooh Bah's "corroborative detail" — makes for theatrical effectiveness. If horses are to be brought onstage after a supposed hard run, they should not look "perfectly fresh": Gilbert interrupts his parody of *The Courier of Lyons* with a "NOTE FOR THE MANAGEMENT," explaining that, if the horses had first been sponged with warm water, "they would have steamed in a natural and effective manner," (July 16, 1870, 21).[19] Sharing the widespread Victorian concern with verisimilitude in art, Gilbert speaks as the future director who would journey to Portsmouth to examine the *Victory* before staging *H. M. S. Pinafore*.

Psychological probability was a more profound concern, and it was far more difficult to achieve than realistic staging. Repeatedly the characters in Gilbert's parodies confess an utter absence of motivation. In Henry Leslie's adaptation of a French source, *Rouge et Noir*, a servant takes a note from a lady, saying, "For no particular reason, I shall suppress it" (January 26, 1867, 205). The reason, of course, is not the character's but the author's: the letter must be suppressed in order to complicate the plot. Gilbert makes this criticism explicit in his parody of John Oxenford's *East Lynne* (adapted from the novel by Ellen Wood), after the husband learns that his wife has eloped: "I will not run after her, for I might catch her as she has only been gone a few minutes, and that would spoil the plot. I will simply tear my hair. *[Simply tears his hair]*" (February 17, 1866, 223). Whatever struck Gilbert as "melodramatic and stagey"[20] was spotlighted in the parody. When English ladies turn up on the coast of Newfoundland in Act III of *The Frozen Deep*, by Wilkie Collins, they openly discuss the questions which the dramatist wants the audience to ignore. "Why did we come here?" Clara asks, and Lucy replies, "Oh, I don't know!" The answer is in the contriving brain of the playwright. His characters have come in order to create a "sensation" scene:

CLARA. — . . . Suppose we should come across the explorers from the North Pole! Wouldn't that be a coincidence?
LUCY. — It would indeed. Ha! Here they are!
Enter LIEUTENANTS CRAYFORD, STEVENTON, *and* OTHER EXPLORERS
LIEUT. C. — Lucy! You here? Who *would* have thought of seeing you? How dedo?

(November 17, 1866, 101)

Given Gilbert's assumption that the theater should offer rational entertainment, the exposure of authorial contrivance was a natural function of his parodies, for a playwright's tricks might be overlooked in a performance. After parodying his own comedy, *Randall's Thumb*, Gilbert noted that the excellent acting "appeared to blind the audience to the defects of the play, and indeed almost give an air of probability to the most farcical incidents" (February 11, 1871, 57). Writing for an audience that seemed eager to accept exciting improbabilities and simplified characters, Gilbert did not always live up to his own standards, but he could at least point out some of his own defects. He called the ingénue of his first comedy "ridiculously-innocent," and he exaggerated an undertone of the play which the audience might ignore. In the parody, the hero (the young lover, at any rate) says, "I will do anything for money. Indeed, every one in this piece (as far as I can judge) would do anything for money" (*An Old Score*, August 7, 1869, 225). On the pages of *Fun*, if not on the stage, Gilbert's characters could speak as if they were already inside the Palace of Truth, acting with the forthright avarice of the couples in *Engaged*. They might be mercenary, but at least in the parody no one could accuse them of acting for "no particular reason."

The parody reviews mark an early triumph of Gilbert's critical and comic awareness. Historically, they are an achievement in overcoming restraints which, by his own report, made the "contemptible character" of dramatic criticism at this time "almost proverbial" ("In the Matter of the Glowworm," January 27, 1866, 198). The restraining influences included the theater manager's power to revoke the free pass of a hostile reviewer and to stop advertising in the reviewer's journal. Personal ties — the reviewer's acquaintance with the actors (a "tetchy race of men") and the fact that "all the principal dramatic critics are dramatic authors" — made honest criticism still more difficult. Writing unsigned parodies gave Gilbert more freedom than regular reviewing, mainly because parody was a less direct, less personal form of criticism. When the playwright was a friend, like T. W. Robertson, Gilbert could call the work a "capital piece" in a postscript, but only after exposing the chief signs of theatrical contrivance in *Caste*, such as the climactic scene when Polly uses song and dance to prepare Esther for her husband's unexpected return: "Ha!" says Esther, "I see from the nature of your dance that D'Alroy escaped from the Sepoys. . . ." "We must have our joke," Gilbert apologizes in the postscript (May 4, 1867, 80); but the joke reveals the stagiest elements in his friend's comedy.

When the playwright was a rival and near enemy, such as F. C. Burnand,[21] Gilbert could use irony to ridicule the play without appearing any more hostile than he had been in reviewing Robertson's *Caste*. A long postscript looks at first like high praise: he calls Burnand's *Deadman's Point* a "very amusing little skit on the absurdities of the Modern Sensation Drama" (February 18, 1871, 73). Then ironies begin to show through: the "skit" would have succeeded perfectly, he writes, had not part of the audience insisted on taking it seriously. Since Burnand's play was produced at the Adelphi Theatre, long noted for sensational melodrama, the serious expectations of the audience were only natural. They had come to enjoy thrilling stage effects — the illusion of a man struggling against overwhelming waves beyond the lighthouse; they had not paid to have that illusion destroyed by faulty machinery. (Gilbert praised this episode as a "Comic Storm at Sea" — an "admirable caricature.")

Other reviewers, who deplored the shoddy production and the hackneyed plot, reported the total failure of Burnand's venture into melodrama: "The performance was received generally with jeers and coughing; the passages intending to be serious being, as a rule, only successful in awakening laughter."[22] But Gilbert told an opposite story, ending with an ironic jibe that must have taxed Burnand's sense of humor: "The management, imbued, no doubt, with some of MR. BURNAND's infectious drollery, revived the system of box-keeping brigandage [charging special fees for box seats], which had long been in abeyance at this house, and succeeded in taking the audience completely by surprise. They seemed to enjoy the joke very much. Altogether, the burlesque is undoubtedly MR. BURNAND's best."

Beyond the strategic success of the parodies, they are a triumph because they show, rather than simply report, the weaknesses of a production. Through the technique of telescoping an action into a handful of lines, the parody of Wilkie Collins' *Black and White* transforms a scene of intended suspense into a moment of farcical absurdity. At a tense moment, the principal characters converge on the hut where Ruth, the mysterious quadroon, lies dying:

COUNT. — What can this Ruth want with me?
MISS M[ilburn]. — *(appearing at secret door)* — What can the Count want with Ruth?
STEPHEN. — *(appearing at hole in roof)* — What can Miss Milburn want with the Count?

(April 24, 1869, 71)

Compressing a whole play into one page of *Fun* is like speeding up a reel of film at a movie. Losing their burden of passion and mystery, the characters jerk about like puppets. Through this technique, all contrivances of plotting and staging become glaringly obvious, and Gilbert makes them still more apparent by letting the characters talk about them. Their self-consciousness gives a devastating end to the parody of Tom Taylor's *Lesson for Life*, when Gilbert ridicules the effort to achieve an impressive stage picture. In this "pretty" piece, "too goody-goody in sentiment," an erring son falls penitent at his father's feet; and the heroine enters with graceful assurance: "A tableau of two? Most inartistic! Let me join you. The pyramidical is the only true form of composition!" (January 19, 1867, 195).

These reminders of artifice point to Gilbert's basic achievement in the parody reviews. In short space, he manages to offer a comprehensive vision of the interplay between illusion and reality in a dramatic performance. His view takes in the whole theater: the characters and the actors, the author, the stage designer, the stage machinery, and the audience. For Gilbert, humor arises when the real elements upset the illusion. On the crudest level, reality intrudes when the stage machinery misbehaves, as it did during the prison scene of Henry Falconer's Irish melodrama, *Oonagh; Or, the Lovers of Lisnamona.* Here the villain, Fardourougha, played by the author, says:

But stay — I will reveal all!
[Is about to reveal all . . . when a ground cloth to be used in the next scene makes a premature appearance from the back of the stage, and cuts all the performers off their legs.]
FARD. — *(recovering his balance)* I will reveal ALL!

[Same business. — All pick themselves up, and go on as if the phenomenon was a familiar characteristic of all condemned cells.]
FARD. — I will reveal ALL!
[Same business. They all hurry off, and reveal ALL in the Green Room.]
Scene 2. *[Behind the Scenes. FARDOUROUGHA and STAGE CARPENTERS discovered. But no — this scene is too awful.]*

(December 8, 1866, 131)

Straining to maintain the stage illusion, against terrible odds, the actor-playwright-villain becomes a ludicrous figure, caught at the point where fiction and reality intersect. In the same parody, another element of the non-fictional scene intrudes: after hearing seventy-one witnesses during a trial, the Judge says:

No, hang it all — I know it's in your part, but — dash it. You know — I can't stand it. Even *they (indicating audience)*, who can stand a good deal, can't stand it!
AUDIENCE. — We can't. Hear! Hear!

(*Fun's* regular critic reported yells of "No more" and "ironical cheers" during the four and three-quarter hour performance.) The parody works because it reflects the whole scene within the theater, including the audience and the stage carpenters, not simply the painted scene upon the stage.

Exploring more subtle contrasts between illusion and reality, Gilbert juxtaposes the identities of characters and actors. His ridicule of the first death-bed scene in *East Lynne* is savage, partly because the scene is sentimentally conceived, but also because Miss Avonia Jones, in the leading role, apparently disregarded the comfort of the child who was playing Lady Isabel's son. The boy lies at the brink of death, not knowing that the governess is his own mother in disguise.

WILLIAM — I have no recollection of my real mother.
LADY I. — Ha! My own boy! *[Clutches at the dying child.]*
WILLIAM — Oh Miss Jones, don't — you hurt me!
LADY I. — Nay, it is in the part.

After momentarily dropping their stage roles, actor and actress carry the scene to its grotesque end:

WILLIAM — Oh that I could see my own mother! I have no recollection of her, and she is dead, but still I should like to see her.

LADY I. — You would? Ha, ha! Behold! *[Pulls off her wig and spectacles.]*
WILLIAM — Ha! *[Dies in great agony.]*

(February 17, 1866, 223)

Finally, Gilbert calls attention to the most subtle illusion of all: the sense of an ending at the close of a well-made play. When Lady Isabel reveals herself to her husband, who has remarried, the Curtain takes control of the situation: "This is getting very awkward. The family arrangements are becoming so extremely complicated, that I think I had better come down."

Such admissions of contrivance typify the humor of the parody plays. As a source for comedy, the contrasts of fact and illusion appealed to Gilbert throughout his long career of ridiculing stage conventions. The parody plays lead directly to his first successful works for the Victorian stage — his series of "extravaganzas" burlesquing grand opera and his "entertainments" for the German Reeds' Gallery of Illustration. In the "entertainments," especially, he would continue to explore the incongruous "multiple identities"[23] of actor and character, and to manipulate the illusions that are created when, by mistake or disguise, a character assumes new roles within a play.

III   *Operatic Burlesques and German Reed "Entertainments"*

Produced between 1866 and 1869, while the Bab ballads and the parody reviews appeared in *Fun,* Gilbert's five operatic burlesques were his first successes in the theater.[24] An opportunity to step beyond the limits of comic journalism came late in 1866, when T. W. Robertson, knowing his friend's skill at parody, recommended him to Miss Herbert, the manager of St. James's Theatre, who needed a new piece for the Christmas season. In less than two weeks,[25] Gilbert wrote *Dulcamara; or the Little Duck and the Great Quack,* an "Eccentricity" (as it was called in the program) based upon Gaetano Donizetti's comic opera, *L'elisir d'amore* (1832).

Parody of another comic work is never apt to be very pointed, and *Dulcamara* is the mildest of Gilbert's operatic burlesques. Its narrow claim to significance now lies in its foreshadowing of the magic potions in *The Sorcerer* and *The Mountebanks*. The sharpest ridicule within the piece is directed not at comic opera but at its own genre. In defining the world of burlesque, Gilbert dissolves illusions as adroitly as he does in his parody reviews. When Belcore enters and asks to be told "where I am, and who are these," Tomaso makes everyone aware of the conventions governing burlesque:

> You're in a village during harvest time,
> Where all the humblest peasants talk in rhyme,
> And sing about their pleasures and their cares
> In parodies on all the well-known airs.
>
> (9)

The characters then suggest that public taste is responsible for these absurd conventions. In order to please the audience, "Each speech must have a pun in it, with very foolish fun in it"; they must screech comic songs, "And laughter to enhance, you know, each song must have a dance, you know. . . ." When the characters request an encore for "these syllables astonishing" ("Hunky-dorum doodle diddle cum day"), the audience is forced to acknowledge some responsibility for fostering the nonsense at which it came to laugh. As in the parody reviews, Gilbert's vision of the absurd extends beyond the footlights.

The note of comic self-consciousness distinguishes his extravaganza from those of his greatest predecessor, J. R. Planché (1825 - 71), who wrote scores of them, punned untiringly, and chafed less than Gilbert at writing lyrics for existing melodies.[26] Both Planché and Burnand, the new master of burlesque in the 1860's, lacked Gilbert's distance from the genre; they apparently never questioned the public taste for "foolish" verbal fun and breakdowns. But Gilbert could see that everyone involved in a performance — author, audience, actors — was assisting in the ridiculous. From this special perspective two decades later, he would give Margaret her explanation of the alleged madness of Sir Despard and his "evil crew" in *Ruddigore*: "They sing choruses in public. That's mad enough, I think!"

As a satirist of operatic convention, Gilbert came into his own with the production of *The Merry Zingara; or the Tipsy Gypsy and the Pipsy Wipsy* (1868), a "whimsical parody" of Michael William Balfe's *Bohemian Girl* (1843). (Gilbert echoed the title of the popular Italian version, *La Zingara*, first produced in London in 1858.) While the burlesque has the usual puns and pleas for applause, at least two reviewers felt a satiric thrust in the humor, which would further distinguish it from the good-natured jesting of Planché and Burnand. A colleague on the staff of *Fun* found Gilbert exposing absurdities in "the most unmercifully humorous way": "The forced hilarity of supernumeraries who turn winecups topsy-turvy before drinking — the spic-and-span condition of the costumes after a lapse of twenty years — the superhuman benevolence of a heavy father — the ceaseless gushings of a long-lost daughter — all these necessities of the lyric drama have been remorselessly caricatured by Mr. Gilbert" (April 4, 1868, 46). Calling Gilbert a "determined iconoclast," the reviewer for the *Illustrated Times* sensed the satiric motive still more clearly. It made him feel that Gilbert "hates 'humbug' of all sorts with a ferocity that is not of this planet. He loves to bowl over the shams, the unrealities, and the insincerities. He cuts at his pet dislikes with a keen pen and an honest hearty hatred."[27] Both critics understood what later students of Gilbert have sometimes ignored: parody can become a form of satire.

In parodying *The Bohemian Girl*, Gilbert was attacking the conventions and clichés of melodrama; and Balfe's hack librettist, Alfred Bunn, had used them all. The parody is designed to rob each melodramatic device of its power to create a sensation. The details noted in *Fun* help achieve this end, as does the Count's realization, when Devilshoof runs off with his daughter, that a quick move might spoil the plot:

COUNT *(reproachfully)* Now, Devilshoof, this is extremely wrong!
    To lose my little baby much mislikes me.
    Pursue him! Stay; a slight objection strikes me,
    Why, we should catch him — all would then go wrong!

The Count's nephew has the answer: "Well, in the opera they sing a song." At this point in *The Bohemian Girl*, they do, in fact, sing a chorale *("andante religioso")*, invoking divine assistance, before dashing off in pursuit of the kidnapper. Because Devilshoof gets away, the Count's daughter can grow up as a young gypsy, and Act III can end with another sensation — the discovery scene when she rejoins her father. Gilbert parodies this stock device less exuberantly than he had done the year before in *La Vivandière*, a burlesque in which an Englishman with sixty-six strawberry marks is told that he is not the rightful Earl of Margate ("No peer of Margate, young, old, short, or tall,/Had ever any strawberry marks at all"); and a quick-witted Italian guide wins the title by saying, "I have no strawberry marks" (69). In *The Merry Zingara*, the heroine has only a small scar, which she thought was from an innoculation. No more proof is needed, however, for the Count possesses total credulity:

COUNT	Anticipated joy half drives me wild!
	Say, were you once a little child?
ARL[ine]	I was!
COUNT	A girl?
ARL.	A very little girl!
COUNT	Do you remember how each morning you,
	When quite a baby —
ARL.	Yes, I do, I do!

                                                            (102)

In addition to the fun with the recognition scenes (Gilbert adds one to the two already in Bunn's libretto), the parody exposes the simplifications of character in opera and melodrama. By romantic convention, a heroine's beauty reveals her virtue: "That girl, so young, so beautiful, commit a robbery? Impossible!" says the Count in the opera.[28] Gilbert expands the Count's remark:

COUNT.	(*aside.*) My code is simple, based on first impressions [,]
	I formed it on a recent case at Sessions.
	Always convict the ugly and the sooty ones;
	Caution the plain ones, and let off the pretty ones.
	(*Indignantly*) That nose a thief's? What nonsense to advance!
	Those eyes steal anything — except a glance!
	To such a charge — although it may be true —
	My virtuous indignation answers "Pooh!"

                                                            (100)

For audiences accustomed to melodrama, first impressions are trustworthy: they can spot the villain as soon as he walks on stage. The parody shows how risky it would be to apply this convention to daily life. But conventions prove useful to the writer who wants strong stock responses to his characters. Bunn makes the Count appear "superhumanly benevolent" in Act I so that his later sorrows will evoke sympathy, if not tears, when he sings *("con expressione di dolore")* "memory is the only friend that grief can call its own . . ." (Act III). Gilbert demolishes the Count's benevolence by grotesquely extending it just at the point when the infant Arline has been rescued from a stag in the opera (a pig in the burlesque):

COUNT (*fondling* ARLINE) I love this very best of pipsy-wipsies,
       (*shakes hands with* DEV.) I've a particular respect for gypsies,
       (*shaking hands with* HUNTERS) Hunters I worship, as I said before,
       (*shaking hands with* FLORESTEIN) I love all nephews, (*kisses* BUDA)
          Nurses I adore;
       Mankind at large I love, my heart's so big —
       (*sees pig*) I'm also very fond of sucking pig.

                                                     (82 - 83)

Gilbert's burlesque characters are not victims of ruling passions; they always have room for other concerns — for sucking pig or tarts, as Miss Treherne discovers while dressed in mourning in Act II of *Engaged*. Their powers of reason are never as overcome by emotion as convention demands. When the Mephistophelean villain of Gilbert's *Robert the Devil* (1868) identifies himself as a "saint by choice, a devil by compulsion" ("Oh, a policeman," someone remarks),[29] he makes an easy denial of moral responsibility. In Giacomo Meyerbeer's opera, *Robert le diable*, Satan can be blamed for the villain's evil; but Gilbert puts the blame on the librettist. The "compulsion" is the librettist's need to elicit thrills from his audience, to rival the Incantation Scene in Karl Maria von Weber's *Der Freischütz*, and to provide excitement with another demonic Samiel or Mephistopheles. This need is the real force behind the villain's daily crimes. Gilbert would not depict anyone as a spectator of his own moral life without making the character ridiculous, as he does when Dame Courtland in *His Excellency* (1894) reports the "perpetual antagonism" between her "Diabolical Temper and Iron Will": "I wish they'd settle it one way or the other."[30] In Gilbert's view, a person with genuine identity makes choices; but the conventions of melodrama can obscure this fact by stereotyping characters and by making them slaves to the author's sense of what his audience wants. To the satirical young dramatist in the 1860's, these wants must have been difficult to respect, especially if he agreed with one of his own characters: "From the point of view of the satirist, the audience is always degenerate."[31]

From a practical viewpoint, however, Gilbert had to please the audience in order to succeed in the Victorian theater. His apparent "contempt" for the public hindered his efforts to write "well-considered comedies," George Meredith believed;[32] and, until such contempt was exorcized, Gilbert would need to master the difficult art of "laughing at his audience without their perceiving it."[33] A critic in the *Examiner* found him doing so, "though it is certainly a defect in a satire that those satirized are wholly unaware of the fact. . . ." At the threshold of Gilbert's busiest decade as a playwright, the field open to his talents must have seemed limited. He was turning away from one genre that he had mastered, and he ended his last operatic burlesque, *The Pretty Druidess* (1869), with Norma's apology for it:

> We have, no doubt, contributed our mite
> To justify that topic of the age,
> The degradation of the English Stage.[34]

Other genres that might have attracted the talents of a comic dramatist were farce and domestic comedy, but Gilbert disliked slapstick, and the second of his two farces in 1867 *(Highly Improbable)* is richer in political satire than in horseplay; and neither piece was considered significant enough to be published. In view of his esteem for T. W. Robertson, domestic comedy was a natural alternative; but Gilbert's first effort in this genre, *An Old Score* (1869) displeased him with its construction and its stereotyped ingénue. Even Robertson in his later works failed to satisfy Gilbert's demand for probability and realistic characterization. Had Gilbert been able to meet his own standards for domestic comedy, how could he have pleased an audience that looked for poetic justice and idealized heroes and heroines? And where in the Victorian theater could he move beyond burlesque and still use the talents as a satirist, versifier, and parodist that he had developed in writing for *Fun*?

One place was the German Reeds' Gallery of Illustration, the snug theatre-in-disguise where plays were called "illustrations," the audience a "gathering," and the roles "assumptions," and where the middle-class bias against the stage was lost in an atmosphere of complete respectability.[35] Here Gilbert first met Sullivan in 1869, two years after the composer had written his first comic opera, *Cox and Box,* with the libretto adapted by F. C. Burnand from John Madison Morton's popular farce.[36] For the minute company of actors led by Mr. and Mrs. German Reed and Arthur Cecil, the tenor comedian, Gilbert wrote six pieces: *No Cards* (March 29, 1869), *Ages Ago* (November 22, 1869), *Our Island Home* (June 20, 1870), *A Sensation Novel* (January 30, 1871), *Happy Arcadia* (October 28, 1872), and *Eyes and No Eyes* (July 5, 1875).

This series far from monopolized his energies during this most prolific span of his career as a dramatist (over thirty works for the stage in six years) — the period of such early successes as *The Princess* (1870), *The Palace of Truth* (1870), and *Pygmalion and Galatea* (1871). But the German Reed pieces have special significance in pointing toward the themes and the situations that Gilbert developed in the operas with Sullivan. *Our Island Home*, for example, contains a prototype of the Pirate King; *Happy Arcadia* suggests the mock-pastoral setting of *Iolanthe* and contains an "Identity Quintette" that is more confusing than the mathematical one near the end of *The Gondoliers*; and *Ages Ago* has portraits that come alive as in *Ruddigore*.[37] And one of his German Reed pieces, *A Sensation Novel, in Three Volumes,* is the culmination of his art as a parodist; in it, he may have "pursued the mind of his day" more deeply into its fantasies than in anything else he ever wrote.

The operetta was far from being the first parody of sensation fiction. Ever since the publication of *The Woman in White* (1860) by Wilkie Collins and *Lady Audley's Secret* (1862) by Miss Braddon, *Punch* and *Fun* had ridiculed the genre. Watts Phillips had written a parodic play, *The Woman in Mauve* (1866); and Gilbert had contributed "A Sensation Novel, by a Small Boy" to the Christmas number of *Fun* for 1866, after publishing a burlesque sensation drama, "Sir Rockhart the Revengeful" (*Fun,* November 11, 1865). But this new parody went farther into the fantasies of his day by showing in its opening where fantasies are made — in the mind of the sensation novelist. The action occurs while the novel is being written, beginning after the end of the first volume when the Author summons the assistance of the Demon of Romance. After each of the first two volumes, and before the last chapter of the final one, the characters come on stage to criticize the novel; they re-enact parts of it and worry over the fates designed for them by the Author's "arbitrary will" (133).

The Pirandellesque complexities of the drama have been illuminated by Jane Stedman in her introduction to Gilbert's German Reed plays. Each character is aware of at least two identities. First, each remembers himself in mortal life, where he committed the "crime" that results in his punishment as a character in a sensation novel. The stock roles grate against their inclinations: a benevolent gentleman has become Sir Ruthven, the bad baronet; an overly indulgent mother has become Rockalda, the *femme fatale* of "no less than 75 sensation novels" (135); a youth who frequented music halls has become "the Author's good young man," Herbert, the heroic

Sunday-school teacher. Their function as stock characters occupies most of their existence, and theirs is a form of slavery to the Author and to the conventions which enslave him. But, during the respite between volumes, they enjoy moments of true identity when they can express their own feelings and imagine what would happen inside the novel if they were free. The good young man would marry the *femme fatale* (who would prefer being respectable); and the innocent governess (that "ridiculously insipid creature," as Herbert calls her) would marry the bad baronet: "I hate mild and amiable men! I like a handsome rover, a scapegrace, a moral brigand, who sets all law at defiance" (164).

Through the contrast between convention and impulse, the parody forces the audience to look at familiar episodes of Victorian melodrama in a radically new light.[38] When the governess insists on re-enacting the scene in which she was seized by the baronet in a pine forest, she reveals something far different from horror: "it was rapture." Her words in the novel only express what convention demands:

ALICE.   Unhand me, coward, or my shrieks shall bring those around you who will make you repent the day you laid a hand on old John Grey's daughter, help! help! help!

HERBERT. *(rushing forward and seizing* SIR RUTHVEN*).* Monster! unhand that lady!

ALICE.   There! *(Aside)* You were always interfering when you were not wanted, just as we were getting on so comfortably together.

HERBERT. Well, it's the Author's fault — *(resuming.)* Monster! unhand that lady! Alice, has he dared to offer violence?

(142)

If Gilbert's audience remembered Alice's distress the next time they witnessed a melodrama, their response was apt to be tinged with amusement. Certainly the dénouement of *A Sensation Novel* would give them cause to sense the artifice of typing characters to fit a melodramatic plot. Gilbert's characters rebel against the Author, forcing him to resurrect the baronet (who had beheaded himself with a hatchet) and to allow them all to marry as they please in the last chapter. Even Gripper, the inept detective, deprives the Author of his last chance for a sensational revelation where he refuses to let himself be revealed as the baronet's abandoned granddaughter (a fate all the more grotesque because Gripper was played by the massive comedian, Corney Grain).[39] The play ends with a complete triumph of personal identity over the roles demanded by convention. When the characters take the plot into their own hands, they challenge the whole mythology of romance and melodrama. The lucky discoveries and rescues of sensation fiction fostered a simplistic view of providence as a force actively engaged in making good people rich and happy. Indeed, Miss Braddon justified the happy ending of *Lady Audley's Secret* as an imitation of providence, even though it resulted from her astounding manipulation of circumstances and the sensationalist's technique of withholding crucial facts until the last moment. Providence was to melodrama what the Good Fairy was to pantomime. Poetic justice was feasible only if good characters were carefully separated from evil ones: this separation encouraged audiences to project their faults upon the villain, rather than recognize them in characters like themselves. Through the hero and heroine, the audience could indulge in wish-fulfillment and the belief that suffering leads not only to romantic union but also to financial prosperity: in Arthur Jones and G. R. Sims' *Silver King* (1880), the reformed hero becomes a millionaire.

The patterns of romance must have affected the audience's sense of reality. As a fictional example, the youth in Joseph Conrad's *Lord Jim* lived "in his mind the sea-life of light literature. He saw himself saving people from sinking ships. . . . He confronted savages on tropical shores, quelled mutinies on the high seas, and in a small boat upon the ocean kept up the hearts of despairing men — always an example of devotion to duty, and as unflinching as a hero in a book."[40] Jim was, after all, heroic in appearance, "clean-limbed, clean-faced, firm on his feet" (31); and, by the laws of Romantic convention, he should have been heroic in character. Appearances were so crucial that Marlow felt betrayed, even angry, because Jim's actions had not equaled his looks: "He had no business to look so sound" (31). The pattern of moral experience was supposed to be simple; for, as we have observed, good looks meant good character; and good character meant, in the long run, good fortune. The financial rewards of a Victorian hero encouraged the successful Englishman to see this pattern in his own life and to persist in his habit of "idealizing every simple feeling, desire, or achievement. He could not believe his own motives if he did not make them first a part of some fairy tale."[41] For those who believed the fairy tales of melodrama, prosperity was simply the reward of virtue.

Gilbert criticizes this convention by distorting its foundations. His characters in *A Sensation Novel* confuse the neat patterns of romance: the hero falls for the woman who corresponds to the "terrible mother"; the anima is sharp-tongued and masochistic ("worry me, harry me"), preferring the alleged villain to the hero: it is as if Andromeda had rejected Perseus for the monster. The baronet and the hero have no real grounds for combat, and neither pair of characters has any special case for poetic justice. In this work of psychological topsy-turveydom, the archetypal figures become humanized; they have plausible motives and self-awareness as they struggle against bondage to their conventional roles.

The play is like an exorcism, allowing archetypes to step outside the mind into common daylight, where they can be laughed at, or faintly pitied, for once, instead of idolized or feared. Seeing absurdity in romantic figures does not necessarily mean rejecting them, for Gilbert went on to write such melodramatic works as *Dan'l Druce, Blacksmith* (1876 — based on George Eliot's *Silas Marner)* — and *Brantinghame Hall* (1888). But laughter can foster a saner attitude toward them — a recognition that their true home is in fantasy where success and failure can be clearly defined. They are not to be mistaken for the complex, unpredictable persons who inhabit the world beyond the limelight of imagination.

IV The Plays of the 1870's: Fairy
Comedy and Serious Drama

While achieving success, in miniature, at the Gallery of Illustration, Gilbert was establishing his reputation in the major London theaters. He began the decade with still another burlesque, *The Princess,* opening at the Olympic in January, 1870, a "respectful perversion" of Tennyson's poem. Gilbert used the original not as a target but as a frame for satire upon the question of equality between the sexes.[42] The "Theatrical Lounger" (possibly Gilbert himself) hailed it as the culmination of his efforts to write burlesques with literary merit: "I honestly believe that Mr. Tennyson would be the first to acknowledge the cleverness of Mr. Gilbert's work."[43]

After a comic opera in May, *The Gentleman in Black,* with music by Sullivan's friend Frederic Clay, Gilbert wrote the first of his "fairy comedies," *The Palace of Truth,* which opened at the Haymarket Theatre in November. This "remarkable success"[44] was another derivative piece, heavily based upon Madame de Genlis' narrative, "Le Palais de la Vérité." But Gilbert took in it a decisive step away from parody and burlesque into a form of drama in which human deceitfulness could be satirized directly, rather than through the ridicule of stock literary types. The fantasy in the story — the magic spell that prevents lying — opened a vein of comedy which Gilbert followed for most of his subsequent career. By 1882, William Archer could report that "His most successful works have all for their scene an imaginary Palace of Truth, where people naïvely reveal their inmost thoughts, unconscious of their egotism, vanity, baseness, or cruelty."[45]

In subdued form, the motif had already appeared in Gilbert's work before he wrote this fantastic play: in "The Folly of Brown," a depraved "General Agent" naïvely complains of Brown's foolishness in refusing to invest his fortune in a joint-stock company, and something like the Palace of Truth had been the scene of the parody plays. In the parody of Gilbert's own comedy, *An Old Score*, one of the women becomes fantastically frank in accepting the proposal of the wealthy Mr. Casby: "Take me away and marry me as soon as you like. *(slyly)* You had better make haste, for Parkle and Manasseh [an elderly lawyer and a moneylender] are both bachelors, and I might change my mind" (August 7, 1869, 225).

The difference in *The Palace of Truth* is that the characters do not realize what they are saying: every cutting remark is accompanied by a polite smile and a gracious gesture. Once the court moves to the palace where lying is impossible without a talisman, a normally servile courtier damns the princess's singing: " 'No voice — no execution — out of tune —/Pretentious too — oh, very, very poor!' *(applauding as if in ecstasies).*"[46] The contrast dramatized Gilbert's abiding concern with the discrepancy between the person and his persona. The same contrast appears in *A Sensation Novel*, only in it the persona was imposed by the Author, and, like a literal mask, it could be lifted. In this play, the mask is the character's own creation; it is so much a part of himself that he never escapes from it entirely, even within the magic Palace.

Had all the characters been courtiers, the play would hardly have moved beyond farce. But at the center of the action is the romance of Prince Philamir and the Princess Zeolide, and the question is what will happen once the effusive lover and the demure princess have to speak truthfully. Their experience raises the implication, later examined by Henrik Ibsen and Conrad, that society depends upon a "saving lie." In another story, Madame de Genlis had written that "l'amour n'est qu'une illusion";[47] and in Gilbert's source she personified truth as a frightening goddess: "mortal eyes could not support her presence in every incident of life. . . .[48] In the Palace, "truth

destroys all sweet and innocent illusions, as well as dangerous errors;
she here wears so savage a form, so pitiless, so hard, so rude, that she
wounds and disgusts even where she might be useful."

For the lovers in the play, the visit to the Palace is a trial by ordeal.
They reverse their roles inside the Palace: Zeolide loses her Victorian
modesty and becomes passionately outspoken, and the Prince
changes from a Romeo to an egoist like Thackeray's George
Osborne. After Zeolide says that she hopes her ardent words have
pleased him, he answers: *"(with enthusiasm)* Pleased me? They've
done more —/They've gratified my vanity, and made/Me feel that I
am irresistible!" (192). The Prince becomes totally divided between
the meaning and the manner of his behavior: with an "affectionate
gesture," he confides to the Princess that she bores him. Gilbert
heightens his vanity, for in the original Philamir was good-hearted
and genuinely in love with Zeolide before coming to the palace. In
the play, he admits that he only courted the Princess to feed his self-
esteem and that he never loved her in more than "an off-hand way"
(193). He illustrates the cynical line which Gilbert deleted from the
later editions: "it is/Unusual for men to love at all."[49] His egoism
grates against his gallant manner: the dissonance is very like what
Clara Middleton would learn to hear from Sir Willoughby Patterne
in *The Egoist* (1879) by George Meredith.

The play stops short of depicting love as an illusion. Zeolide's love
stays genuine, even when the Prince horrifies her; and she steps
aside for her rival like the proper self-sacrificing heroine of Victorian
mythology. But the Prince's character is an obstacle to the success of
the ending; for, by magnifying his vanity, Gilbert closed off the op-
tion given him by the source in which the narrator insists that
Philamir never stopped loving Zeolide even when he turned to Mirza,
her scheming rival. In Gilbert's play, Philamir must make a more
sudden change from a mere liking to an ardent love of the Princess.
The King offers an easy way out by handing him the talisman that
would allow him to lie once more and to assure Zeolide that he loves
her. But he professes love without the talisman, and romance stands
the ordeal. Aside from this, however, the ironic implications are enforced by the ending. When the Palace loses its spell, everyone is
relieved: "We shall get on much better." The lovers in the subplot
are not reunited; the King begins lying again about his conjugal
fidelity; Philamir grows effusive about his feelings; and Zeolide,
after her scenes of grand passion, reverts to her old modesty: *"(very
demurely)* I love you, Philamir — be satisfied!"

The mingling of irony and romance characterizes the tensions within Gilbert's "fairy comedies" during the early 1870's. Working against the romantic motifs, the magical exposure of hidden feelings invites a wary view of human nature. The farcical *Creatures of Impulse* (1871) suggests that repression of basic impulses is universal: a magic spell brings out aggressiveness in a coward, coquettishness in a prude, and fear in a soldier. This pattern is confused when a miser becomes compulsively generous under the spell, but the effect of the play is to stress once more the divergence of outward behavior and inner impulse.

Where magic does not expose human failings, the fairy comedies bring them to light through the use of a naïve point of view. In *Pygmalion and Galatea,* the heroine values life so much after being transformed from a statue to a person that she cannot rationalize any form of killing. To her, a soldier is a "paid assassin";[50] shooting a fawn is an act of murder. She is shocked to learn that in society she must practice false modesty, concealment of her feelings, and irony: "Is it possible/To say one thing and mean another?" (60). Her attitudes change from delight to disillusionment: "life is bitterer to me than death" (85), and she willingly turns back into stone. On a larger scale, Galatea's reversal of attitudes is worked out among the fairies in *The Wicked World* (1873) when they find their society disrupted by the intrusion of three men from earth. Their passion for the men leads to possessiveness, jealousy, hatred, and rage: they behave much like the women in the fable at the beginning of Meredith's *Ordeal of Richard Feverel* (1859): peace ends once a man comes to their island. It returns to Gilbert's fairyland only with the men's departure and the fairies' rejection of sexual love.

Because the focus rests upon suffering, sentiment dominates *The Wicked World,* as it does *Pygmalion and Galatea,* in which the pathos of the naïve heroine is central to the drama. The fairy comedies become increasingly sentimental, until in *Broken Hearts* (1875) Gilbert drops the word "comedy" from the title page. In this tearful play about four women who have withdrawn from the world of men, the comic element has shrunk to the form of a humpbacked dwarf, who is too full of self-pity to be very amusing. Traces of farce linger only in the scenes in which Prince Florian, invisible in a magic cloak, tricks the ladies by speaking for the lifeless objects they adore. He is the masculine intruder on "The Island of Broken Hearts" where the women channel their affections toward a favorite thing — sun dial, mirror, fountain — much as Laura does in Tennessee

Williams' play, *The Glass Menagerie*. The intrusion of a real lover
upsets their world and leads the most naïve of them to heartbreak
and death. The ending is in stark contrast with Gilbert's first resolution of this motif: in *The Princess*, the men lead Ida and the girl
graduates out of Castle Adamant into the normal world where they
can marry and bear children.

Heavy sentiment makes *Broken Hearts* one of Gilbert's most difficult works to read "with the same spirit that its author writ." His
blank verse had been reasonably clean in the earlier plays; now it is
clotted with adjectives, especially when the heroine watches a
"silent solemn shadow" and speaks as if she were moved by her own
pathos:

> Yet even this calm rest — this changeless peace,
> Saps my poor fragile fabric day by day,
> And the first shaft that sorrow aims at it,
> May shake its puny structure to the ground![51]

Gilbert's attitude in writing the play invited sentimentality, for he
wrote to Clement Scott: "I have been so often told I am devoid of a
mysterious quality called 'sympathy' that I determined in this piece,
to do my best to show that I could pump it up if necessary."[52] He
was in no mood to smile when Burnand called it "Broken Parts."

Despite sentimentality, the play illuminates both the theme and
the form of Gilbert's fantastic dramas. "Whimsical allegory" was the
label he adopted for *The Princess*, and in some degree the fairy plays
are all written in an allegorical mode. One reviewer complained that
Gilbert was "much too fond of allegory": in *The Wicked World* and
Broken Hearts, "at every turn, Symbol is sought for in the dialogue.
And the characters are built upon perfect symbolical principles.
Hawthorne, in his stories, does the same thing."[53] Without preten-
ding to see the symbolical principles as clearly as this reviewer did,
we may still grasp the central theme of Gilbert's allegory. It concerns
the barriers to an open relationship between men and women. The
barriers are symbolized by the castle walls of *The Princess*, the
remote cloudy home of the fairies in *The Wicked World,* and the
women's island retreat in *Broken Hearts*.

Within the characters, one barrier is the Victorian ideal of
feminine purity, if not of sexual ignorance. Zeolide's demure manner
conceals her passion, and she fills the role that society has set for her.
When Mirza tells her that "people call you cold/Because you are so

cold to Philamir," she answers, "Why, Mirza, he's a man!" (179). How else could a proper young lady act? Her passivity frustrates the Prince, yet he encourages it by his own attitude toward women. With true priggishness, he rebukes a coquette for displaying her ankle: "one who shows her cards so candidly/Will not supplant the Princess Zeolide" (197). "Man hath no appetite for proffered love," says the false knight in *The Wicked World* (42).

Women in these plays are caught, therefore, in a double bind: they must conform to the ideal of purity, living in semi-ignorance of sex; yet they must respond to a man's advances if they are to escape spinsterhood. Because Jenny Northcott in *Sweethearts* (1874) is unable to confess her love — "it seems so shocking for people to talk about such things,"[54] — she lives unmarried for thirty years afterward. Faced with confusing masculine demands, Gilbert's women might well feel most at home in a remote castle, on a cloud, or on an island where they can love anything but a man.

The lesson of tolerance for "mortal man" in *The Wicked World* points directly to *Charity* (1874), an embryonic problem play which invites sympathy for a woman, Mrs. Van Brugh, who has had a child without being legally married. This unpopular drama carries a strong attack on the double standard of sexual morality, and it shows that idealizing women is one way of enforcing the standard: a woman's pedestal was so high that there could be no climbing back after a fall. The pharisaical villain, Mr. Smailey, expresses the respectable viewpoint: "society . . . has decided that a woman who has once forfeited her moral position shall never regain it."[55] The bitterest scene comes when he confronts Ruth Tredgett, a reformed tramp-woman whom he had seduced twenty years before:

MR. S.   . . . Remember, Tredgett, I am a person of influence here, and a
         county magistrate —
RUTH.   What, d'you sit at quarter sessions?
MR. S.   Certainly.
RUTH.   And sentence poor prigs?
MR. S.   Yes. Why do you ask?
RUTH.   Nothing; go on — it's all topsy-turvy!

(107)

The double standard helps make society into Topsy-Turveydom. (Gilbert's play with this title, another failure, was produced in the same year.) Moral incongruities are stressed in *Charity* by the high status of the Smaileys: the father is a country gentleman, and the avaricious son was played by W. H. Kendal, who normally appeared in romantic roles. Against their respectable selfishness, the tramp-woman stands as an exemplar of charity beside the heroine, Mrs. Van Brugh, and Dr. Athelney ("a Colonial Bishop-Elect"). The audience's own respectability may have kept it from sympathizing with the heroine (though the *Graphic* blamed Gilbert's obscurity for this failure);[56] and the scriptural ending must have taxed the patience of anyone who came to the theater for entertainment. Even the actors burst out laughing on the terrible night when a papier mâché plate fell from the wall and rolled on edge across the stage just as Dr. Athelney was about to say, "the greatest of these is CHARITY!"[57] But no one could doubt that the author's sympathies were for Mrs. Van Brugh and that he counted himself among those men who would be as "hot in the defense of an insulted woman as in the days gone by . . ." (125).

As a dramatist, Gilbert's chivalric defense of insulted womanhood culminates in *Gretchen* (1879), his treatment of the Faust theme, which he ranked with *Broken Hearts* as his finest work. As early as "Only a Dancing Girl" in 1866, his serious writing tends toward the vindication of insulted women against the censure of a hypocritical society. An important allusion to that poem supports the theme of Anne Edwardes' novel, *Ought We to Visit Her?*;[58] and Gilbert's adaptation of her work for the stage opened two weeks after *Charity*. *Gretchen* is the most direct treatment of this theme of the fallen woman, for the woman's "fall" is definite and part of the action, not an obscure event in the past, as it is in *Charity*. The seduction itself is not viewed as a fatal sin within the play; aside from the scorn of the village girls, what upsets Gretchen is the discovery that Faust, her seducer, is a priest. Before this discovery, she could say, "Heaven is kind to me, for all my sin!"; and imagine herself as Faust's wife, "When thou and I may face the world again."[59] When she learns who Faust is, she leaves him and begins to die as mysteriously as Samuel Richardson's Clarissa. Defending the play in 1885, Gilbert oversimplified his heroine by asserting, with childlike certainty, "As a matter of fact, Gretchen dies of a broken heart because Faust has seduced her."[60] (In the same year Ko-Ko would document such deaths with "Tit-Willow.") But in Gilbert's treatment of the legend, the seduction would not have caused heartbreak had there been no barrier to her eventual marriage. As Gilbert depicts his heroine, the loss of virginity has no effect on her moral character: she stays kind and charitable, suffers no madness, gives way to no suicidal impulses, and dies as triumphantly as her counterpart in Gounod's opera. In terms of Gilbert's chief value — charity — her fall has been insignificant.

V   *Farcical Comedy: The Impact of* Engaged

In cynical counterpoint to these dramas of feminine heroism are the plays of the 1870's in which Gilbert fulfilled his promise as a satirist. Aside from the first five libretti Gilbert prepared for Sullivan (*Thespis*, 1871; *Trial by Jury*, 1875; *The Sorcerer*, 1877; *H.M.S. Pinafore*, 1878; *The Pirates of Penzance*, 1879), at least two comedies stand out among his major achievements. These are *Tom Cobb* (1875) and *Engaged* (1877), which Gilbert called "farcical comedies" and which seemed to the critics to be like *The Palace of Truth* in realistic guise. The characters reveal their selfishness as complacently as if they were inside the magic Palace, but the scene is contemporary England. Charity and tolerance have little value in these plays: what matters to the characters, above all else, is money. There are no masculine intrusions into realms of feminine purity, for the women equal the men in cunning and in avarice. Unlike the ladies who worship sun dials and die of broken hearts, the jilted women of the comedies launch breach-of-promise actions and retain only a veneer of passion, like Angelina in *Trial by Jury*:

> *Oh, see what a blessing, what love and caressing*
> *I've lost, and remember it, pray,*
> *When you I'm addressing, are busy assessing*
> *The damages Edwin must pay!*

The breach-of-promise suit epitomizes the theme of these plays. In the conflict between material and romantic goals, love and altruism give way to a driving urge for financial security. In little bursts of self-revelation, this urge breaks through romantic pretensions. The high-strung heroine of *Tom Cobb* illustrates the dominant motive without betraying the slightest awareness that her shrewdness threatens her assumed role. After corresponding with a poetic major-general and becoming engaged to him by telegraph, she reports that "now, for eighteen months, no crumb nor crust of comfort has appeased my parched and thirsty soul! Fortunately my solicitor has all his letters."[61] In her world, money can heal the wounds of the most romantic spirit: "The huckstering men of law appraise my heart-wreck at five-thousand pounds!" Later, when she thinks she has found her major-general, she kneels at his feet, "*kiss-ing his hand as she places the writ in it.*" Three ladies consider breach-of-promise actions in *Engaged* in which even the rustic Scots woman tells Cheviot, "There's a laddie waiting outside noo, to serve the bonnie writ on ye!"[62]

In relying upon legal machinery, these injured women contrast still more strongly with Mrs. Van Brugh (who is extremely naïve about marriage settlements) and the ladies on the Island of Broken Hearts. The comic women use social institutions to gain their ends; but the pathetic ones flee society once they are injured: Mrs. Van Brugh leaves England for a new life in some colony; Hilda and Vavir retreat to their fantastic island; and Mrs. Theobald, stifled by respectable society in *Ought We to Visit Her?*, returns with her husband to a vagabond life in the theater. The comic women resemble their creator in fighting for their own interests: Gilbert's legal squabbling was becoming a habit by this time; and the heroine of *Tom Cobb* saves letters, as Gilbert did, for future evidence. They follow the teaching of the Comic Physiognomist: "The great object in life is to be first at the winning-post." But the women maintain the pretense of being forced into the contest, and they fight as if legal weapons had been pressed into their delicate hands.

The comic incongruities of both plays stem from this pretense. The pretended role is conventional: romantic, altruistic, benevolent, according to the character — "Why," asks Tom Cobb, "do benevolent people have such long hair?" (230). The character's persona comes from outside — from sentimental literature, the theater, and the morality that stresses duty and self-sacrifice. Opposing the assumed role is the desire for financial success: the lower-middle-class setting of both plays gives this motive crucial importance. *Tom Cobb* opens with the hero contemplating suicide because of his debts; Cheviot Hill considers suicide on hearing that his investments have failed in *Engaged*. The title of that play suggests the *cash-nexus* binding the principal characters, as well as the web of ambiguous engagements for marriage. Cheviot is at the center of the financial net, for Belvawney's income of one thousand pounds a year depends upon Cheviot's remaining single; and Miss Treherne will marry Belvawney only if he can secure his income. If Cheviot marries, Mr. Symperson will receive it instead of Belvawney. But Symperson's daughter, Minnie, refuses to marry Cheviot until she can be certain that his investments are safe. Marital and financial concerns are so interwoven around Cheviot that no one can separate them.

The task of Symperson and the two ladies is to emerge prosperously from this financial tangle without losing the masks that they have chosen for themselves. Miss Treherne has chosen the role of a woman of great emotion, but she is determined not to make an imprudent marriage. Though she loves Belvawney "madly, passionately," she reminds him that "business is business, and I confess I should like a little definite information about the settlements" (45). Mr. Symperson plays the role of a benevolent father and uncle, while Minnie acts the "superhumanly innocent ingenue,"[63] whom Symperson calls his "lamb" and "little dickey-bird."

No foolish sentiment, however, stops Minnie from breaking the engagement the minute she hears of Cheviot's financial ruin: "Well, upon my word. There's an end of *him!*" When Symperson protests, Minnie justifies her decision without quite dropping her innocent mask: "Dear papa, I am sorry to disappoint you, but unless your tom-tit is very much mistaken, the Indestructible was not registered under the Joint Stock Companies Act of Sixty-two, and in that case the shareholders are jointly and severally liable to the whole extent of their available capital. Poor little Minnie don't pretend to have a business head; but she's not *quite* such a little donkey as *that,* dear papa" (77). She would be like Dora Spenlow in *David Copperfield,* if Dora had only read the financial section of *The Times.*

For the Victorian audience, the most arresting clash between the ideal and the practical must have occurred in the first act, which begins like a rustic Scottish idyll. Maggie sings at her spinning wheel in a garden; Angus comes forward and declares his honest love: "I'm but a puir lad, and I've little but twa braw arms and a straight hairt to live by, but I've saved a wee bit siller — I've a braw housie and a scrappie of gude garden-land — and it's a' for thee, lassie, if thou'll gie me thy true and tender little hairt!" (41). The scene promises rural melodrama, with a villain lurking somewhere to try to spoil their romance. Gilbert's own melodrama of the previous year, *Dan'l Druce, Blacksmith,* contains a similar episode in which the young hero comes to the forge to tell Dorothy that "I have loved thee, boy and man, for ten years past; and I shall love thee, come what may, through my life. . . . it's my heart that's speaking now and not my tongue."[64] Angus stays just as earnest; but, after he receives the blessing of Maggie's mother, *Engaged* changes in one sentence from potential melodrama to satiric comedy:

ANG. *(wiping his eyes).* Dinna heed the water in my ee — it will come when I'm ower glad. Yes, I'm a fairly prosperous man. What

wi' farmin' a bit land, and gillieing odd times, and a bit o' poachin'
now and again; and what wi' my illicit whusky still — and throwin'
trains off the line, that the poor distracted passengers may come to
my cot, I've mair ways than one of making an honest living — and
I'll work them a' nicht and day for my bonnie Meg!

(42)

Angus speaks as if he had stepped inside the Palace of Truth, but
in this play no one is shocked at his revelation. Money justifies every
action. The satiric point is stated by Mr. Symperson, who fails to see
that it applies to himself: "What a terrible thing is this incessant
craving after money!" (78). By ingeniously pursuing it, Angus
becomes a parodic Scots cousin to the vital rogue-heroes of Dion
Boucicault's Irish plays. In *The Colleen Bawn* (1860), Myles-Na-
Coppaleen poaches and keeps a still, but he is genuinely kind
hearted, able to restore a peasant girl to the squire whom she had
secretly married: "Take her, wid all my heart."[65] Angus also resigns
his sweetheart, after Maggie succumbs to the attractions of Cheviot's
wealth: "Maggie, if she married me, would live in a nice house in a
good square. She would have wine — occasionally. She would be
kept beautifully clean." But Angus receives compensation: "it's a'
for the best; ye'll be happier wi' him — and twa pound is twa
pound" (52). The transaction destroys the last vestige of the rustic
idyll.

Such a mixture of parody, satire, and farce was a challenge to Victorian audiences. Reviewers were divided in their responses, and the
public did not give *Engaged* a lengthy run.[66] Gilbert contributed to
the general confusion by insisting that it be "played with perfect
earnestness and gravity throughout. . . . the characters, one and all,
should appear to believe . . . in the perfect sincerity of their words
and actions."[67] This directive was so important to Gilbert's humor
that his Hamlet, in *Rosencrantz and Guildenstern (Fun*, 1874), lec-
tured the players upon the same point: "he who doth so mark, label,
and underscore his antick speeches as to show that he is alive to their
absurdity seemeth to utter them under protest, and to take part with
his audience against himself."[68] His advice apparently ran counter to
the habits of British comedians (the players summarily reject it), and
it was not completely followed by the actors in *Engaged.*[69] To the extent that it was followed, his audience was challenged not only to
detect parody but to grasp the intent of a dramatist who masked his
humor with seriousness. *The Times* reviewer sensed the parody of
stock characters, but he confessed that he could not find Gilbert's

main intention;[70] and another critic left the theater with the "uneasy impression that Mr. Gilbert has intended to satirize something or somebody unknown."[71]

The basic responses included both horror at Gilbert's cynicism and delight (or boredom) with his nonsense. One reviewer considered the play a "picture of humanity more cynical than has been seen since the days of Swift."[72] To another, the satire seemed totally destructive; for, instead of "correcting certain faults or frailties," it condemned human nature "altogether as wholly despicable and bad."[73] Looking back some years later, Augustin Filon asserted that: "So cruel a farce had never been seen. The public was accustomed to two or three comic characters, to satire at the expense of two or three ridiculous types. Here was a caricature of all mankind. The spectators laughed, but the jest was too bitter for their palate. It was at once too bitter and too true."[74]

The truthfulness of the jest could be debated, but the reviewers who were shocked by it must have sensed that *Engaged* touched upon painful facts of Victorian life. With financial scandals receiving prominent notice in the daily papers, they could hardly deny the existence of a massive *cash-nexus* in English society. *The Times* complained of how the craving for money encouraged irresponsible speculation, and even chided women for demanding such expensive clothes and carriages that men were tempted to neglect morality and prudence in pursuing wealth.[75] Trollope's satiric novel *The Way We Live Now* (1874 - 75) attacked the "commercial profligacy"[76] which had helped bring on a worldwide depression in 1873. The novel was criticized for the same faults as *Engaged:* "We can look in vain for any nobleness of character to compensate for all the rascality against which we rub shoulders."[77] Both works deprived their audience of the satisfaction of identifying with characters who were at once virtuous and successful; they implied, rather, that virtue was a rarity, and something quite unlikely to win financial dividends.

But several critics found nothing at all offensive in *Engaged.* Sharing Lewis Carroll's view of the play as "a good bit of extravagant nonsense,"[78] they had no need to react defensively; it seemed too remote from daily life. Though the *Times* reviewer reported his distaste for Gilbert's humor, he wrote that "To call such a piece cynical is idle, for that it is to be taken seriously no intelligent person would care to suppose."[79] The object of its satire is not humanity, said Moy Thomas, who found it full of "much amusement of a harmless kind."[80] The bored critic for the *Saturday Review* saw it as innocuous parody of Wilkie Collins' sensation novel, *Man and Wife* (1870, dramatized in 1873), noting that the bewildering plots of both works turn upon a Scottish marriage. Rather than voicing horror, he complained that the play was tiresomely long and hardly original.[81]

Which response does justice to *Engaged*? It is an anomalous work, more satiric than pure farce, and more consistently ironic than comedy of manners. It anticpates Oscar Wilde's *The Importance of Being Earnest*, as critics have noted: Miss Treherne's appetite for tarts matches Algernon's taste for muffins, and Symperson's mourning for Cheviot suggests Jack's assumed solemnity in Act II after killing off his fictitious brother. But *Engaged* is more grotesque: the characters are too low in the middle classes for comedy of manners; the financial stakes count more for them; and Symperson is not playing makebelieve when he dons his mourning clothes: he really wants his nephew to commit suicide.

Gilbert maintains greater irony than Wilde, and greater distance between the characters and the audience. When Miss Treherne devours a tart while reporting her miseries, no one comments on the incongruity; in *The Importance of Being Earnest*, Jack asks how Algernon "can sit there, calmly eating muffins when we are in this terrible trouble" (Act II). No one in *Engaged* keeps saying "It's absurd," as Jack and Algernon do. Jack invites the sympathies of Wilde's audience, and Algernon (through his wit) wins at least admiration; but Cheviot, neither witty nor well-meaning, can only invite sympathy because he is handsome and finally successful. Because the play is so thoroughly ironic, the offended critics cannot be blamed for taking it seriously and, in self-defense, for charging Gilbert with cynicism.

But the critics exaggerated the cynicism by failing to recognize one function of irony: to invoke a norm by calling attention to its absence. George Bernard Shaw overlooked this function when he praised his *Arms and the Man* (1894) by contrasting it with Gilbert's "barren . . . cynicism, pessimism, and irony" in *Engaged*. Shaw claimed that his own comedy had a "positive element," a "happy ending with hope and life in it," while *Engaged* is "nothing but a sneer at people for not being what Sergius and Raina play at being before finding one another out."[82] Shaw misses the point by assuming that Sergius and Raina, on romantic pedestals, represent Gilbert's moral norm. Frederic and Mabel in *The Pirates of Penzance* are what Sergius and Raina play at being, and they are thoroughly ridiculous. The characters for whom Gilbert shows the most sympathy are honest and charitable: they are not conventional paragons of romance. Mrs. Van Brugh and Gretchen are not immune to temptation; the plaindealing Mrs. Theobald loses patience when her young admirer gets "upon moral stilts": "It isn't the right and wrong of the thing [the fact that he loves her], it's the absurdity of it that takes away my breath!"

If Gilbert sneers at the characters in *Engaged,* he does so not simply because they are selfish but because they keep up a pretense of romance or benevolence while battling tooth and nail for money. The contrast between the women in this play and the ones in *Broken Hearts,* as well as the similarities between the opening scene and part of Act II of *Dan'l Druce,* may have been what prompted one reviewer to suggest that Gilbert was parodying his own works.[83] But, if he were, the parody need not be nihilistic. Echoes of Gilbert's serious plays could remind the audience of the need for charity, in contrast to the over-prizing of money and one's own image. In this way parody brings together the two worlds of Gilbert's romantic and satiric vision. It allows human foils — persons with conscience, self-knowledge, and feeling — to stand just off-stage from the compulsive role-players in this farcical comedy. Sensing the contrast allows for laughter and removes the grounds for charging the satirist with representing life as if there were no alternatives to the selfishness of Mr. Symperson and Cheviot Hill.

VI *Conclusion: Accepting the Two Worlds*

In dramatizing the tensions between romantic ideals and social experience, Gilbert states the conflict most clearly in the song from *Princess Toto,* which is quoted at the start of this chapter. The "world of dreams" and the world of "sin and sorrow" occupy his imagination simultaneously. Princess Toto tries to break away from the flawed world by forgetting the past and leaving society. Her quest for a world to match her dreams leads her farther and farther from social restraints — first, to a life among brigands, and finally to a tribe of Indians: "you are quite primitive, and unconventional, and all that?" But the Indians are only her father and his court in disguise, and she never achieves her wish "to revel in the society of barbarous man in all his primitive magnificence" (Act III). She is a ludicrous romanticist, an adolescent Madame Bovary; yet her key song invites sympathy for her viewpoint. If dreaming really could erase folly and "every sad mistake," "How very, very, few indeed/Would ever keep awake!"

While Princess Toto tried living as if dreams could achieve these impossible ends, Gilbert himself wrote plays that were designed to awaken his public to the illusions concealing reality. His fantasies bring the audience to a palace where masks become transparent; his parodies, such as *A Sensation Novel*, reveal how literary conventions can stylize and oversimplify our pictures of experience. His almost forgotten serious plays — *Broken Hearts*, *Charity*, and *Gretchen* — focus on the consequences of sad mistakes, on suffering and loss, and on the importance of charity in human relationships. These works give weight to the message in one of Bab's flippant asides:

> (We must not be severe:
> We have our failings, all;
> For none are perfect here
> On this terrestrial ball.)[84]

CHAPTER 3

The Gilbert and Sullivan Operas

I N retrospect, few developments in Gilbert's career seem more inevitable than his work as a librettist. His first published verse was a translation of the laughing song from *Manon Lescaut*,[1] and he began writing for the stage at a time when the field of light opera was virtually empty of significant English works. As early as 1861, a critic remembered Alfred Bunn's hackneyed libretti for Balfe's operas and imagined, by contrast, a collaboration that foreshadowed Gilbert and Sullivan's: "Oh! shade of BUNN . . . only fancy a libretto so excellent in every respect that its author is positively called for with the composer on the first night! . . . If not indelicate, PAN begs to assure all inquiring musical friends that he is a poet . . . and that his terms, though enormous, are perfectly commensurate with the merits of the article produced" (*Fun*, December 14, 1861, 131). "Pan" sounds like Gilbert himself, and the monogram for this article may be his.[2] As a member of the *Fun* staff, he would have shared the general scorn for Bunn and the concern for making English opera a rational form of entertainment. Given his talent for parody, he no doubt seconded T. W. Robertson's wish that "operatic burlesques," such as Burnand's and Frank Musgrave's *Windsor Castle*, would "become naturalized among us" (*Fun*, June 24, 1865, 59).

In France, this form of entertainment was flourishing in the work of Jacques Offenbach, whose operas won Gilbert's intense admiration. He translated and adapted the Frenchman's *Les Brigands* in 1871, hoping to prepare a text that would be suitable for an English production; and earlier, in the days when Englishmen had to cross the Channel to see such things, he confessed his interest in the most popular of Offenbach's operettas. "*Orphée aux Enfers* is the special treat that Y. O. C. [Your Own Correspondent] always promises himself whenever duty or pleasure takes him to Paris. . . ."[3] Gilbert's delight was surely in Offenbach's catchy tunes as well as in the irreverent wit of the French librettists. His taste for light opera at this time gives the lie to the legend that he could not distinguish "God Save the Queen" from "Rule, Britannia."[4] Moreover, in the operatic burlesques of the 1860's, he wrote lyrics to fit melodies by Offenbach, Donizetti, and even Bellini, winning praise for his musical taste: his "selection of music, because it is superior to the music-hall trash of the period, is over the heads of the audience."[5]

Certainly Gilbert's ear was sensitive enough to the elegance and verve of Sullivan's music for *Cox and Box* when he reviewed the "triumveretta" in 1867. But he also detected a quality in the music which would threaten the equal relationship of librettist and composer once their careers merged: "Mr. Sullivan's music is, in many places, of too high a class for the grotesquely absurd plot to which it is wedded. It is funny here and there, and grand or graceful where it is not funny; but the grand and graceful have, we think, too large a share of the honours to themselves."[6] Given the choice of partners, Gilbert might well have preferred Offenbach to the man whose training in church music and oratorio and whose ambition to write grand opera would clash with Gilbert's practical sense of what the comic theater required.[7]

With the right composer, comic opera offered Gilbert the chance to use the best talents he had shown in his first decade as a writer. It allowed him, first of all, to combine his proven gifts as a "doggerel bard" with his skill as a playwright. Except for the one-act *Trial by Jury*, his libretti are compromises between opera and regular drama. The mixing of songs and dialogue falls in the tradition of John Gay's *Beggar's Opera*, but Gilbert's works are more "operatic" because of their long passages in verse for soloists and chorus. Many of his songs possess a unity of their own, and in at least one of his early musical plays, *No Cards*, he simply lifted a Bab ballad and used it as a lyric.[8] With his stockpile of Bab ballads and other verses for *Fun*, the temptation to use ready-made lyrics must have been great; but, for all his self-borrowing, Gilbert normally avoided using his early verses in the operas.

While his most famous songs can sometimes stand alone, they gain by being heard in their dramatic context. At the same time, they enrich and widen the world of the operas. When Sir Joseph Porter stops the action of *H. M. S. Pinafore* to tell the story of his professional success, he at once characterizes himself and deepens the work's satiric themes. His shameless egotism — "I always voted

at my party's call,/And I never thought of thinking for myself at all"
— makes him sound like a captive of the Palace of Truth. He is so
under the spell of his self-importance that he has lost all sense of his
absurdity. For the original audience, the topicality of the song linked
Sir Joseph with W. H. Smith, the bookseller whom Disraeli made
First Lord of the Admiralty.

On a wider level of implication, the rise of an office boy to "the
top of the tree" was a caricature of the myth of the self-made man,
one which Dickens had satirized with Mr. Bounderby in *Hard
Times*. In retelling the myth, Sir Joseph spoke to the aspirations of
his Victorian audiences, especially to those Americans who flocked to
the theaters when *Pinafore* was the rage in a nation of self-made
men. Through unconscious irony, Gilbert forces any thoughtful
listener to recognize the arrogance and complacency inherent in the
idea of being self-made. Once the action is resumed, Sir Joseph's
story provides a basis of his conduct — for his fanatic insistence upon
equality, which turns out to be a way of putting all men on a level
beneath himself. Like a good Bab ballad, "When I was a lad" reveals
an ironic world; but the song has a chorus as well as a narrator, and
its ironies are part of the larger world of ironic contradictions within
the opera.

As a librettist, Gilbert could make the fullest use of his talent for
stylizing life. This talent had given distinction to the absurd figures
in his comic drawings; stylization allowed him to condense a Victorian melodrama into a one-page parody in *Fun* and to transform a
breach-of-promise suit into a page of comic opera, the first version of
Trial by Jury.[9] Verse could save Gilbert so many words, as anyone
can tell by comparing the opening of *H. M. S. Pinafore*, of *The
Mikado* or of *The Gondoliers* with the exposition scenes of his prose
plays. The conventions of opera, ridiculous or not, sanctioned
sudden expressions of feeling ("Oh horror!" "O ciel!"), quick
changes of heart, and asides: operatic emotion could be stylized, and
conventions provided the formula for it. Convention also allowed
Gilbert to merge masses of people into units — sisters, cousins, and
aunts, or gentlemen of Japan; and the effect of their postures and
synchronized movements is not unlike that of the patterned lines in
Gilbert's sketches of crowds for "Down to the Derby" and "The
Half-Crown Day."[10]

Finally, music could add to Gilbert's work what he had tried
desperately to "pump up" in *Broken Hearts* and had totally avoided
in *Engaged*. Music could stir feeling — joy, sadness, pride, even

tenderness — and restore to the operas the emotional vitality that the librettist apparently forfeited by stylization and caricature. In David Cecil's words, music "makes the fairies in *Iolanthe* fairy-like and the ghosts in *Ruddigore* eerie and Jack Point's love story poignant."[11] In the most unlikely places, it could give the operas sentimental appeal — as when the twenty lovesick maidens briefly return to their "old, old loves again," or when Frederic and Mabel stop being silly long enough to sing "Ah, leave me not to pine" in Act II of *The Pirates*. The right music could intensify the moments of feeling as well as add to the humor in Gilbert's work.

Much depended, however, upon the composer. To collaborate with Frederic Clay (as Gilbert did in *Ages Ago* in 1869 and in later musical plays) or with Arthur Sullivan meant relinquishing even more control over his work than when he entrusted it to actors for performance on the stage. By writing long sections of dialogue and by keeping the concerted numbers to a moderate length, Gilbert retained a strong measure of control in the German Reed pieces and in *The Gentleman in Black* (1870). But, when Clay did have a verse to set, "he broke up Gilbert's lines with incessant undramatic repetitions of words to suit his own melodic phrases";[12] and, according to one reviewer, he appeared "to have no notion of humour." Whenever "the author tempts the musician with a sly bit of fun he refuses to answer to the call." With *Cox and Box* in mind, the reviewer suggested that Clay "take a hint from Mr. Sullivan's eccentric scoring."[13]

As a composer who imitated the sound of a locomotive in *Thespis*,[14] Sullivan had the requisite humor and audacity for comic opera. Furthermore, when setting a text, he maintained "the integrity of his librettist's syntax."[15] Even the music for "The Lost Chord" begins with rather extreme fidelity to the rhythms and phrasing of Adelaide Procter's verse. The words dominate the melodic line — with its repetition of the same note — almost as much as they do in Sir Joseph's chanted announcement that he is "the monarch of the sea." Sullivan's habit of repeating notes in a musical phrase might have been fostered by his settings of biblical texts, where he wanted each word to be heard clearly, as in the first section of "How many hired servants" from *The Prodigal Son* (1869).

But with a sometimes slavish respect for audibility and syntax, Sullivan also had the talent for bringing out the full meaning of a sentence by stressing key syllables and by imitating "the inflections of the voice" through rises and falls in tone.[16] At his best, he makes Gilbert's words far more expressive than they sound when merely spoken. The difference can be felt by trying to read the first stanza of "Were I thy bride" without thinking of the melody, or by contrasting "He is an Englishman!" when spoken, with Sullivan's splendid emphasis on the verb: the Boatswain sounds overwhelmed with the sheer "isness" of the fact:

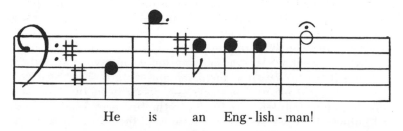

He   is   an   Eng-lish-man!

At such moments, and in almost every patter song, Sullivan gives language a hyper-expressiveness, a power to say more than spoken words ever can. (What speaking voice would leap an octave to stress an "is"?) While exaggerating the tempo and the changes in pitch, he remains essentially true to the inflections and phrasing of animated speech.

As if this gift were not enough, Sullivan brought still another talent to comic opera: his skill at musical parody. Being nearly as sensitive to the absurdities of operatic convention as Gilbert, and apparently feeling genuine scorn for at least one popular operatic composer,[17] Sullivan parodied Handel and Donizetti in *Trial by Jury;* and he echoed the famous Incantation Scene from Weber's *Der Freischütz* when John Wellington Wells summoned the spirits in Act I of *The Sorcerer.* It was Sullivan's idea to end that act in the style of Italian opera, with the principals leaning over the footlights, "arms outstretched towards the gallery."[18] The humor and ingenuity that he brought to the collaboration more than compensated for the new limitations on Gilbert's freedom as a writer.

These limitations included the need to consult the composer on the plot for a new piece (with his original idea sometimes being rejected or modified); the writing of alternate versions of the same lyric to give more freedom to the composer, who could reject a song altogether, just as Gilbert could and a few times did reject Sullivan's settings.[19] Finally, there was now the chore of attending musical rehearsals, where Gilbert had to learn the rhythms and tempi of the numbers in order to plan the stage business. These requirements made the operas the genuine fruit of a collaboration, but they also created ample opportunities for conflict between librettist and composer as the years went by.

With Sullivan's contribution, Gilbert's work now acquired a lyrical element which flowed in brilliant counterpoint to his usual satiric depiction of individual and social absurdities. This counterpoint gives the operas their distinctive form, setting them apart from earlier ballad operas and later musical comedies. While Gay's *Beggar's Opera* also juxtaposes lyrical and satirical elements, Gilbert's work with Sullivan contains more fantasy, more radical contrasts between romantic melodies and absurd situations, and more elaborate concerted passages — especially in the long and sometimes musically exciting finales to the first acts. When Gilbert and Sullivan fully realized the importance of the chorus in *H. M. S. Pinafore*, the form of their work became one of the surprises of theatrical history; for something like Attic comedy appeared on the London stage. Through the ceremonial structure of the operas and their mixture of fantasy, lyricism, and satire, Gilbert earned a title which is almost oxymoronic: he became the "Victorian Aristophanes."[20]

I *Gilbert's Aristophanic Comedy: Conflicts and Political Satire*

The echoes of Aristophanes are found in the thematic and formal elements of Gilbert and Sullivan. First, their parodies of melodrama and grand opera have a function that parallels Aristophanes' continual ridicule of Euripides. In both cases, the allusions are to a world of immense passions and pretensions, and the tragic or melodramatic world becomes a backdrop for the down-to-earth concerns, the shrewd scheming, and the undignified combats of comedy. *Trial by Jury* is a ritualistic combat between Edwin and Angelina, and the jury takes sides in the breach-of-promise suit just as a chorus might in Aristophanes. In contrast with the pettiness and the courtroom setting is the operatic formality of the combat, a formality enforced by Sullivan's allusions to grand opera, where a heroine's passions are romantic, not financial. Gilbert's self-controlled and rather diminutive characters may stumble into situations that call for magnificent emotions; but, when facing such opportunities for self-sacrifice as confront Ko-Ko, Pooh-Bah, and

Pish-Tish in the Act I trio of *The Mikado,* they generally "object." In pursuing a reasonable, safe way out of their difficulties, they differ from their more rash counterparts in grand opera who become the victims of passion — of all the emotions which Gilbertian characters name so much more often than they feel.

A second Aristophanic theme in Gilbert's libretti is his obsession with conflicting worlds, one of fantasy and one reflecting everyday reality. In expressing this conflict, the action of *Thespis,* the first opera with Sullivan, is so simple that it is ritualistic. Actors invade Mount Olympus, usurp the functions of the decrepit gods for a year, and are finally driven away when the gods return. Gilbert was still building on this pattern at the end of the series, when in *The Grand Duke* another dramatic company gains control of Pfennig-Halbpfennig and creates fantastic political and social chaos until the rightful duke returns to power. Between these two works, the "invasion motif"[21] is central to *Iolanthe,* where British lords blunder into fairyland and then suffer a retaliatory extension of fairy power into Parliament.

The movement into a kingdom of fantasy, where the intruders make radical innovations, can also be clearly seen in *The Gondoliers* and *Utopia Limited.* Baratarian society becomes hopelessly muddled by the two commoner-kings' ideal of equality, and Utopia almost bursts into revolution because the English political and economic advisers (the "Flowers of Progress") make its institutions too perfect for human nature to endure. By showing the effects of an intrusion, the second acts of these operas resemble the second half of a comedy by Aristophanes, where the focus is on the intrusions of impostors;[22] and the movement into a fantastic realm of Barataria, or Utopia, follows the pattern of *The Birds,* where characters from the familiar world venture into the Kingdom of the Hoopoe.

Gilbert's early treatment of the invasion motif in *The Wicked World* afforded the framework for his first genuinely Aristophanic comedy, *The Happy Land* (1873). Written in collaboration with Gilbert à Beckett, this parody of his own play created a brief sensation and was almost immediately censored by the Lord Chamberlain because three actors impersonated the leaders of the tottering Liberal government. Caricatures of Gladstone, Ayrton, and Lowe enter fairyland singing: "Oh, we are three most popular men!/ We want to know who'll turn us out. . . ." So direct a political satire was almost unknown in the Victorian theater. As Bulwer-Lytton said, "the English, instead of finding their politics on the stage, find the

stage in their politics."[23] The Prince and Princess of Wales came and
laughed heartily on opening night (before the Lord Chamberlain
had time to intervene), and the *Graphic* prophesied that the play
would open a "new field" of "extravagant drama."[24]

It did, despite the Lord Chamberlain, if *Pinafore* and *Iolanthe* and
Utopia count as offshoots from *The Happy Land*. But the "new
field" was as old as Attic comedy. The best scene in *The Happy
Land* is an ironic catechism resembling the testing of the Sausage
Seller in *The Knights*, when Demosthenes tries to see if he is fit to
govern Athens:

SAUSAGE SELLER   But I don't know a thing
                   Except my letters.
DEMOSTHENES   Ah, the pity is
                   That you know anything.[25]

In *The Happy Land*, Mr. Ayrton tests the fairies to find a suitable
First Lord of the Admiralty:

MR. A.   What's the average cost of a first-class ironclad ship?
ZAY.   Five hundred pounds.
MR. A.   No. Next. . . .
NEXT FAIRY   Don't know.
MR. A.   Very good, but not quite right. Next. *(to Darine)*
DARINE   Please, sir, a first-class ironclad *what?*
ALL THE MEN   Ship, my dear — ship, *ship*.
DARINE   *(innocently)* Please, sir, what *is* a ship?
MR. A.   Here's a First Lord ready made!

Playful irony later gives way to direct statement as the fairies awaken
to the horrors of democracy (in *The Wicked World*, the horror was
sexual love): they resolve never to try Popular Government again.

Gilbert's later satire relies more upon irony than either *The Happy
Land* or the plays of Aristophanes. His ridicule is far less partisan and
less specific in its targets, inviting several critics — from William
Archer on — to deny that it is true satire.[26] In *H. M. S. Pinafore*,
there is something grotesquely impartial about Gilbert's pointing the
same criticism against W. H. Smith, the First Lord in Disraeli's
Conservative cabinet, that he and Gilbert à Beckett had made
against Gladstone's government five years before. The question of
his satiric intent is additionally complicated by his decision to make
Sir Joseph Porter "a radical of the most pronounced type" in order to

remove "any suspicion that W. H. Smith is intended. . . ."²⁷ This
stratagem may have reassured Sullivan and placated the Lord
Chamberlain, but it could not cover up the analogy between the
prosperous bookseller turned war lord and Sir Joseph, the
businessman with his complacent formula for success: "Stick close to
your desks and never go to sea,/And you all may be Rulers of the
Queen's Navee!" Disraeli himself thought the opera was terrible,
but he reportedly mustered enough humor to call his loyal cabinet
minister "Pinafore" Smith.²⁸

The ambiguity of Gilbert's political humor has led to contradic-
tory views of his politics. David Cecil speaks of his "Liberal" impatience with florid displays of patriotism, while Gilbert's first
biographers assert that he was "at heart a Tory of the most die-hard
description."²⁹ Contradiction is a natural result of trying to
generalize about the politics of an ironist whose *Gondoliers* "confounded" the Socialist, according to Frederick Wedmore in *The
Academy,* but whose next opera with Sullivan was his most vigorous
attack on the British Establishment. *The Gondoliers* proved to Wedmore that "Mr. Gilbert, like most level-headed gentlemen — like
most important minds, one need hardly add — is, in the broad sense,
on the side of the Conservative."³⁰ Yet *Utopia Limited* made fun of
the monarchy and the nobility — "Our Peerage we've remodelled
on an intellectual basis,/ Which certainly is rough on our hereditary
races"; it satirized the injustices of capitalistic enterprise; it glanced
ironically at the problem of poverty ("We haven't any slummeries in
England"); and it won a nearly rave notice — ostensibly on account
of the music and the staging — from George Bernard Shaw, who had
shown only bored contempt for Savoy Opera after the opening of
*The Gondoliers.*³¹ But these contradictions reveal what anyone who
remembered *Iolanthe* might have guessed: the satirist who smiled at
people for entering the world as "either a little Liberal/Or else a little Conservative" does not fit neatly into either party.

What sustains Gilbert's irony and makes his satire seem ambiguous is his vision of Topsy-Turveydom. The vision came clearly
to him in the ballad "My Dream" (*Fun,* March 19, 1870, 15), where
Topsy-Turveydom is a mirror world inverting the normal one. The
ballad was expanded into a satiric musical extravaganza in 1874: the
new piece bewildered the audience and ran hardly a month at the
Criterion Theatre. Its inversions of morality and chronology (people
live backwards in Topsy-Turveydom) were enforced with
Surrealistic stage effects: a chandelier rising from the floor and

tables and chairs suspended "head downwards from the flies."[32] But Gilbert's satiric point had been made in fantasies from Swift's *Gulliver's Travels* to the brilliant ones in his own decade — Carroll's *Through the Looking-Glass* (1871) and Butler's *Erewhon* (1872). These works become satiric when they reveal absurd similarities between fantastic lands and our own. Like Butler's satire, Gilbert's comes from the irony of a naïve person's blindness to the realities of a fantastic land. His satisfied British member of Parliament, Mr. Satis, cannot detect the resemblances between Topsy-Turveydom and England. For the play to have any satiric effect, the audience has to notice what Mr. Satis ignores: it must recognize that Mr. Crapulee's description of Topsy-Turveydom (where "Folly is honoured, wisdom is despised, — disreputable wealth is courted, — honest poverty condemned") fits England more exactly than the member of Parliament's claim that everyone there "is wealthy and happy." Satis's incorrigible Philistine optimism blinds him to every similarity, though Mr. Crapulee warns him that "Extreme[s] meet, and the differences may not be so great as you suppose."[33]

Throughout Gilbert's satire, the fantastic worlds are meant to mirror his society. As one of his fairies remarks, "Great Britain is the type of Fairyland!"[34]; and Great Britain provides the model for the absurdities of Titipu, Barataria, and Utopia. If absurdity seemed inseparable from social existence in Gilbert's vision, then a program for reforming society through satire or political action would have been unthinkable. When the Utopians complain that military reform has ruined the country by making it so strong that war is impossible, and when they consider the sanitary and legal reforms to be a disaster because doctors and lawyers are now out of work, the only remedy is to gratify their masochistic need for disorder. Let them have the ultimate British political institution, government by party: "Then there will be sickness in plenty, endless lawsuits, crowded jails, interminable confusion in the Army and Navy, and, in short, general and unexampled prosperity!" Here is the "muddle" of *Hard Times* and the Circumlocution Office of *Little Dorrit*, greeted by the Utopian populace with shouts of "Ulahlica! Ulahlica!" G. Wilson Knight calls this "a just conclusion," because "the only system that fits a paradoxical world is one that functions in terms of paradox."[35] If in this case "paradox" means "muddle," Knight's statement contains a sobering insight.

Gilbert's skepticism about reform did not mean that he lacked concern about the welfare of British life. The operas supply grotesque images of the ills and weaknesses of the social order, reflecting in miniature a conflict within an established structure of power. Normally, one character represents official authority — the Judge in *Trial by Jury*, Sir Joseph Porter in *H. M. S. Pinafore*, the Lord Chancellor in *Iolanthe*. Because the chorus has such prominence, the action tends to affect the complete society depicted on the stage. The love philter affects a whole village in *The Sorcerer* (marriage, according to Alexis, is the "panacea for every ill"); Sir Joseph's notions of equality disrupt the naval regimen on board the *Pinafore;* and supernatural beings and the Lord Chancellor in *Iolanthe* resolve a political question that had troubled a whole nation. The plot is almost never limited to the problems of the main characters: their difficulties are part of some larger predicament, especially in the last three operas where the emphasis becomes more political than personal, and the theme expresses a concern of Aristophanes — the governing of a state.

While Gilbert never approached Athenian boldness in dealing with public issues and personalities, his libretti often had direct pertinence to the issues of his times. One of the clearest examples is *H. M. S. Pinafore*, written while the nation was divided over the question of whether or not to wage war against Russia in order to preserve a vestige of Turkish power in the Balkans. The winter of 1877 - 78 was the time when the Jingo song rang out in the music halls; and Gladstone, for being horrified at the "Turkish atrocities," found himself threatened by a patriotic mob.[36] Even Disraeli's cabinet had sharp disagreements over the lengths to go in risking war. The joke about Sir Joseph Porter's lack of naval experience enforced a point that critics of Disraeli's "brinksmanship" were quick to cite: England had no military force ready to match the armies of a continental power.[37]

Jingoism was a dangerous way of ignoring this weakness, and Gilbert was surely parodying the bluster of the music halls in the first act finale in which the British tars stand with fists cocked for "a knock-down blow." The upsurge of nationalistic pride also finds mocking expression in the grandiose anthem, "He is an Englishman," based upon the fatuous assumption that a person's nationality is a matter of choice rather than of birth.[38] *Pinafore* outlasted this particular war scare, which was already lessening by the time the opera began its run in May, 1878. But the satire still served a timely end by exhibiting on stage two weaknesses that could have led the nation into a disastrous war — military unpreparedness and blind nationalistic fervor; for both had contributed to the downfall of France in the combat with Prussia eight years earlier. They would lead to more disasters soon after Gilbert's death.

II *The Struggle with the Law*

The vitality of the Savoy Operas, decades and oceans away from their original time and place, suggests an inner strength that is far more potent than topical satire. Part of their life springs from the ritualistic quality they share with the comedies of Aristophanes. The operas appeal to our delight in ceremonial behavior, to the fun of wearing masks, playing games, and watching contests in which the participants must not violate the most inhibiting rules.[39] As the object of a Gilbert and Sullivan cult, the operas in performance have some kinship with an elaborate form of public ritual.

Since the opening nights, when the theater rustled with dutifully turned pages of libretti, there has been a certain solemnity in the public response to these allegedly comic operas. To the "Captious Critic" at the Savoy during the first run of *The Gondoliers,* the crowd seemed "less like an audience than a congregation. They had heard of Gilbert and Sullivan, and had come to worship at their shrine. . . . They offered one another half their books of the words as good people do when you are put into a strange pew at church. What is more, they looked at their books rather than at the stage, and followed the songs with awe, and the singularly wordy dialogue with reverence."[40] More recently, Louis Kronenberger has claimed that the operas appeal to people "with a rather stunted sense of humor"; and Paul Kresh, in an amusing personal essay, treats his addiction to Gilbert and Sullivan as a neurotic obsession.[41] The outrage of a confirmed Savoyard at some departure from the stage business devised almost a hundred years ago suggests that the operas serve a ritualistic need — why else would innovations be so upsetting? Preserved — if not embalmed — by the D'Oyly Carte Opera Company, the Savoy "tradition" has been about as difficult to revise as the Anglican liturgy.

But, from a more charitable viewpoint, the veneration of the operas shows what a vital place they have earned in the public mind.[42] *Pinafore* and *The Mikado* have achieved the ends of folk art by giving people in many parts of the world a common fund of witticisms, images, and cheering melodies. Sullivan, perhaps more than Gilbert, made the operas appealing; and the signs of his achievement grew audible in the public response during his own lifetime.

On opening nights at the Savoy, before curtain rise and between acts, the least fashionable part of the audience would sing their favorite choruses from the gallery — "Hail Poetry!" or "I hear the soft note" — and sing so well that the assembled socialities and even the actors behind the curtain would cheer.[43] There could hardly have been surer proof of the life of these works in the memory and imagination.

The ritual enacted in a typical Gilbert and Sullivan opera involves an intrusion, a resulting crisis, and a resolution marked by a wedding — by weddings *en masse*, to be more exact. Gilbert complicates this pattern in three basic ways. One is by enlisting sympathy for the nominal intruders, as in *The Gondoliers*, where Marco and Giuseppe technically become impostors when they rule Barataria and yet hold the sympathetic interest of the audience. In *Princess Ida*, Hilarion with his friends invades the women's college; but his role is to awaken Ida to sexual love, and he is no more of an impostor than Nanki-Poo, whose intrusion interferes with Ko-Ko's plans for his wedding. Both the Major-General's daughters and Sir Joseph's sisters, cousins, and aunts invade masculine strongholds; but the true impostors are only the Major-General and Sir Joseph, who lack the knowledge that would make them worthy of their rank.

A second variation is the ironic ending which allows the impostors to stay in power, rather than be driven off as they usually are in Aristophanes. Despite the Major-General's lie, he escapes death, thanks to the Union Jack; and the Machiavellian Judge wins a bride, or perhaps a mistress, at the end of *Trial by Jury*. A third complication is the double invasion — sometimes reciprocal, as in *Iolanthe* and *The Pirates;* sometimes simply additional, as in Act II of *The Grand Duke*, where the Prince of Monte Carlo intrudes into a court that has already been taken over by impostors. Whatever its form, Gilbert's invasion plot calls for marching or dancing intruders — pirates in a Gothic chapel, bold dragoons, peers in full regalia, fairies before Westminster Hall, the Mikado and his court, and Sir Despard and his "evil crew." If drama is basically movement,[44] and if Attic comedy developed from ritual processions,[45] then the Gilbert and Sullivan operas contain the primal dynamic of theatrical art.

Ritualistic motifs give strength to the most popular of the operas. According to Northrop Frye, the vestiges of a sacrifical rite, "the king's son, the mimic death, the executioner, the substituted victim, are far more explicit" in *The Mikado* "than they are in Aristophanes."[46] Frye uses this opera to illustrate his belief that "the

element of play" separates art from savagery: Gilbert's plot affords a
way of "playing at sacrifice." Such "playing" occurs in most of the
operas, from the time John Wellington Wells yields to "popular
opinion"and descends through the trapdoor at the end of *The
Sorcerer* to the "legal deaths" by Statutory Duel in *The Grand
Duke*. The threat of execution faces the Major-General and Iolanthe;
and a masked headsman, with axe and block, appears in the Act I
finale of *The Yeomen of the Guard*. *Patience* contains the most comic scene of playing at sacrifice when the poet Bunthorne assumes the
victim's role by putting himself up as a prize in a raffle: he enters
garlanded like a bull or a heifer, led by a procession of love-sick
maidens.

Gilbert handles the motif repeatedly, but in *The Mikado* he dwells
upon it with the most spirit and gusto. The "cheap and chippy
chopper," the snickersnee, and the threat of "something lingering,
with either boiling oil or melted lead," are images which work upon
the nerves and give the opera a strange kinship with the rash of
seriously macabre plays, such as Wilde's *Salomé*, which appeared in
European theaters near the end of the century.[47] Human sacrifice is
necessitated in *The Mikado* by the conflict of two worlds. One is
Titipu, the lax, workaday world of political expediency where
everything, somehow, is "quite correct." Here a public official can
plan to marry his ward without feeling any of the legal scruples that
bother the Lord Chancellor in *Iolanthe*; and all but one of the public
offices can be filled by one man, the versatile Pooh-Bah. Here the
Mikado's stifling decree against flirting can be circumvented simply
by selecting a Lord High Executioner who is already under sentence
of death and therefore " 'cannot cut off another's head/ Until he's
cut his own off.' "

Threatening these ingenious makeshift arrangements are two
forces: romantic love and legal absolutism. Nanki-Poo embodies the
romantic force; his intrusion at the start of the opera threatens but
does not in itself disrupt Ko-Ko's plans for marriage. The larger
threat comes from the seat of legal authority, the Mikado's court. His
decree against premarital flirtation strikes at life itself, threatening
the normal relationships of men and women. The predicament for
the young is almost as distressing as the one in Aristophanes'
Ecclesiazusae ("Women in Parliament") in which law requires a
youth to have intercourse with a hag before mating with a woman of
his choice. The aging Katisha has something of the hag's role as she
stalks Nanki-Poo, and her praise of ripeness and her dispraise of

Yum-Yum's youth restates the conflict in the bitter duet between the
First Hag and the Girl, who fight over a young man in *The
Ecclesiazusae* (11. 893ff.). There is wintry truth in her words to Yum-
Yum:

> Thy doom is nigh,
> Pink cheek, bright eye!
> Thy knell is rung,
> Rose lip, smooth tongue!

As an intruder from the world of absolute law — the law of mor-
tality as well as the law of the Emperor — Katisha is the "ill-omened
owl" who disrupts the merrymaking over the betrothal of Nanki-
Poo. Her voice must be drowned in youthful shouting:

KAT. In vain you·interrupt with this tornado!
     He is the only son of your —
ALL   O ni! bikkuri shakkuri to!
KAT. I'll spoil —
ALL   O ni! bikkuri shakkuri to!
KAT.   Your gay gambado!
     He is the son—
ALL   O ni! bikkuri shakkuri to![48]

Even before Katisha bursts in, the world of absolutes reaches
Titipu through the Mikado's letter demanding an execution. The
letter prompts another makeshift scheme — Ko-Ko's attempt to
bribe Nanki-Poo to become the sacrificial victim: "Observe: you'll
have a month to live, and you'll live like a fighting-cock at my expense. When the day comes there'll be a grand public ceremonial —
you'll be the central figure — no one will attempt to deprive you of
that distinction. There'll be a procession — bands — dead march —
bells tolling — all the girls in tears — Yum-Yum distracted — then,
when it's all over, general rejoicings, and a display of fireworks in the
evening. *You* won't see them, but they'll be there all the same" (28).

But, in the second act, this scheme fails, and Ko-Ko resorts to the
political expediency that marks official life in Titipu. He fakes an execution, and he has it graphically reported to the Mikado in the trio,
"The Criminal Cried." When the alleged victim turns out to be the
Mikado's son, the absolute powers must be propitiated; and, by
courting Katisha, Ko-Ko becomes the real sacrificial victim — her
new "prey."[49] It takes this sacrifice to bring Nanki-Poo back to life:

"while Katisha is single, I prefer to be a disembodied spirit," he says; but "When Katisha is married, existence will be as welcome as the flowers in spring" (58).

Finally, Ko-Ko must propitiate the law itself, personified by the Mikado. He does so by appealing to the tyrant's vast egotism: "When your Majesty says, 'Let a thing be done,' it's as good as done — practically, it *is* done — because your Majesty's will is law." The Mikado is caught in the trap of his own pretensions. Omnipotence rules by fiat, saying, "Let there be an execution," and there is one. Since the Mikado is too self-important to deny himself this power, he has to answer Ko-Ko's logic chopping with "Nothing could possibly be more satisfactory!" The solution allows the young to have their way, and it satisfies the Mikado's demand for an execution. Titipu has survived the invasion of legal absolutism, though the most ingenious of its politicians pays for his success by winning Katisha. With the emblems of Age, Repression, and Death now placated, the revelers can resume the chorus from the Act I finale. They celebrate dawn and life, while acknowledging what Katisha represents: the night that comes too soon.

Music and dance help to make the enactment of this primal combat joyous and playful, but the chief source of the playfulness is in the libretto. The verbal music of alliteration and rhythmic pattern becomes most pronounced when the imagery is grimmest. When Ko-Ko, Pish-Tish, and Pooh-Bah finally describe the fate to which they so strenuously object, the artifice of patterned sounds offsets the grisly appeal to the senses:

> To sit in solemn silence in a dull, dark dock,
> In a pestilential prison, with a life-long lock,
> Awaiting the sensation of a short, sharp shock,
> From a cheap and chippy chopper on a big black block!
>
> (27)

Gilbertian verbal music can be so loud that it calls attention to itself; but, rather than being a blemish, as it would be in serious verse drama, it creates a welcome counterpoint to the painful meanings of the words.

The patterned sounds also increase the esthetic distance from which Gilbert invites the spectator to view the opera. In more direct ways, distance is created by specific references to artifice. The noblemen in the opening chorus explain that they are not Japanese marionettes, despite appearances; and they allude to the glut of

Japanese fans, vases, and jars in late Victorian parlors. Though on the level of setting and costume Gilbert took elaborate pains to achieve an authentic atmosphere, he laced the text with allusions and silly jokes ("it might have been on his pocket-handkerchief, but Japanese don't use pocket-handkerchiefs! Ha! ha! ha!") which destroy the pretense that the opera represents the life of Japan.[50]

But, as the esthetic distance lengthens, the distance between Titipu and England becomes less and less. When Ko-Ko lists the "society offenders who never would be missed" and when the Mikado recites his catalogue of punishments to fit the crime, the stage clearly reflects the world of the audience — Titipu becomes England in kimonos. Each of the patter songs functions like a *parabasis* in Aristophanes: the song interrupts the action but advances the satirist's themes; it is topical and allusive, and it is sung straight to the audience. The effect is like that of a *parabasis*, where the chorus and chorus leader come forward to make a public address.

But, unlike Aristophanes and like most Victorian dramatists, Gilbert was cautious in using personal satire. He knew that Gladstone's handling of the Egyptian crisis, with his hesitancy about relieving General Gordon, was still fresh in everyone's mind. (Khartoum was finally relieved, too late, on January 28, 1885, a month and a half before the opening of *The Mikado.*) But he names no "statesmen of a compromising kind," for "The task of filling up the blanks I'd rather leave to you." The effect of this reticence, however, is to involve the audience even more directly than Aristophanes had done by specific name calling. At such moments, *The Mikado* becomes a "play" in the literal sense; and the spectators are meant to participate in it — to fill in the blanks in Ko-Ko's song, to assist at his staged wooing of Katisha, to sense the dramatic irony of the Mikado's observation that "virtue is only triumphant in theatrical performances," and, finally, to accept the dénouement for what it is: an impossible reconciliation of opposed forces, as unstable as a union of Ko-Ko and Katisha.

The conflicting forces within *The Mikado* appear repeatedly in other operas. In *The Pirates of Penzance* and in *Ruddigore*, melodrama represents the absolutist world of rigid order; and the burlesque of melodrama becomes one with the satire of legalistic behavior. With its subtitle, *The Slave of Duty*, which names the central theme, *The Pirates* is an exploration of moral law — the Victorian ethic of duty and renunciation. Having reached an apotheosis in Carlyle and George Eliot, "duty" was being questioned in the

1870's by skeptical writers. Gilbert had long been fascinated by the power of a concept — if not a mere word — to affect behavior. "Captain Reece" treated the most abject slavery to duty; and *Our Island Home,* an immediate source for *The Pirates,* has an apprenticed pirate who never questions his "dreadful duty" to kill his newly discovered parents. "I am bound to slaughter every prisoner I take. You wouldn't ask me to break my articles?"[51]

As a romantic hero, Frederic in *The Pirates* treats the concept in the same unquestioning way. His world of absolute values clashes with the pragmatic one of General Stanley, who lies to save his daughters from marrying pirates; and it opposes the moral relativism of the Pirate King, who observes that piracy, "constrasted with respectability . . . is comparatively honest" (I, 130). But even the pragmatic characters have some absolute commitments: General Stanley worships his newly purchased ancestors and suffers remorse from dishonoring them with his lie; the pirates have absolute respect for orphans, the Queen, and the Union Jack. Only the policemen resist the temptation to view everything in absolute terms. Experience has taught them how difficult it is to perceive people in distinct categories of good and evil. How can they, when the felon's capacity for innocent enjoyment "Is just as great as any honest man's"?[52] This fact is the ground for their famous complaint:

> Ah! When constabularly duty's to be done —
> To be done,
> A policeman's lot is not a happy one —
> Happy one.
> (164)

The action of *The Pirates* develops the conflict between absolutism and relativism. The central event is Frederic's coming of age, ending his apprenticeship to the pirates, and allowing him to re-enter respectable society. While he sees piracy and respectability as opposites, his view is constantly challenged and ridiculed as the opera unfolds. The King warns him of the "cheating world" of Victorian finance, "where pirates all are well-to-do," and of the hypocrisy in respectable society, where one may "play a sanctimonious part/ With a pirate head and a pirate heart" (130). The Major-General demonstrates this point when he lies about being an orphan: he is as dishonest as the outlaws. The first act ends with a symbolic equation between piracy and British society, as the Pirate King unfurls the Jolly Roger and the Major-General waves the Union Jack.

The equation returns at the end, when the pirates turn out to be peers, the pillars of society, on whom the social climbing Major-General eagerly bestows his daughters. If Frederic has any intelligence, he should conclude that the distance between piracy and respectability is much less than he had imagined. For the audience, the little distance makes the opera an alternative to the world of melodrama, where a cut-throat stays too preoccupied with crime to hear "the brook a-gurgling," and where a policeman's lot is consequently a happy exercise of virtue. *The Pirates* shows our world of moral confusion, and it torments the romantic hero by placing him in such a dilemma that he must betray his beloved in order to perform his duty.

Unless Gilbert intended an irony which is not conveyed by the libretto, Frederic and Mabel differ from the dutiful characters in *Ruddigore* by sincerely believing what they say. Only once do the words suggest humbug — at the moment when Mabel's sisters doubt her reason for accepting Frederic:

> The question is, had he not been
>   A thing of beauty,
> Would she be swayed by quite as keen
>   A sense of duty?
>
>   (137)

This question stays unanswered in *The Pirates*, but in *Ruddigore*, Gilbert's burlesque of melodrama eight years later, the heroine uses a moral code as an excuse for doing as she likes. Rose Maybud is akin to Minnie Symperson in *Engaged,* who decided that it would be her duty "to devote my life, my whole life, to making myself as happy as I possibly can."[53] Duty in *Ruddigore* means obeying one's impulses. Rose exploits the definition: first to justify rejecting the sailor, Richard Dauntless, in favor of his wealthy brother; and then to accept Richard once more, after he reveals that his brother is the rightful baronet, doomed to a life of evil. Neither she nor Richard are moral puppets like Frederic.[54] "Duty" allows Richard to mask self-interest as moral courage. "My conscience made me!" he pleads before the angry villagers in the Act I finale; after he has stopped his brother's wedding with the revelation of his cursed identity:

I knew 'twould blight thy budding fate —
I knew 'twould cause thee anguish great —
But did I therefore hesitate?
   No! I at once obeyed!

(II, 105)

The plot of *Ruddigore* is resolved by a surprising victory of individual assertion. The timid Sir Ruthven (Robin Oakapple in the
first act) eventually musters the courage to disobey the witch's curse
and the ancestral voices that have condemned him to commit a
crime a day. After a lifetime of trying to escape the curse, he makes
his brave resolution: "I *will* defy my ancestors. I *will* refuse to obey
their behests, thus, by courting death, atone in some degree for the
infamy of my career!" With this new sense of integrity, he can sing
an acceptance of his fate in the Patter-Trio:

Now I do not want to perish by the sword or by the dagger,
But a martyr may indulge a little pardonable swagger,
And a word or two of compliment my vanity would flatter,
But I've got to die tomorrow, so it really doesn't matter!

(125)

Had he not gone on to discover the dizzy logic proving that a refusal
to commit a crime was "tantamount to suicide" and therefore ex-
empt, as a crime, from the witch's curse, the opera would have had
to end as *Iolanthe* almost ends — with the execution of a person who
chooses death rather than obedience to law.

The drama of choice is at the heart of *Iolanthe,* the most intricate
and perhaps the most brilliant exploration of conflicting worlds in all
of Gilbert and Sullivan. Fairyland and British politics are the two
alternatives, and almost every element in the opera expresses their
opposition. Scenically, the conflict appears in the two sets: first, "An
Arcadian Landscape," then "Palace Yard, Westminister." Strephon,
the son of the fairy Iolanthe and the Lord Chancellor, is sent from
the first realm into Parliament, burdened with two conflicting
selves: "down to the waist, I'm a Tory of the most determined
description, but my legs are a couple of confounded Radicals, and,
on a division, they'd be sure to take me into the wrong lobby" (I,
237 - 38). As his complaint reveals, the mortal world is itself divided;
for Parliament is split into Peers and Commons; the populace, into
Liberals and Conservatives; and society, into various classes — the
aristocracy, the bourgeoisie (who are supposed to bow to the

marching peers), and the proletarian masses who receive attention in Strephon's omitted song, "Fold your flapping wings" (Act II).

Psychologically the divisions persist in the chief mortal, the Lord Chancellor, whose mind is like a courtroom in which his romantic self pleads against his official conscience and persona. After finally deciding to marry his own ward, Phyllis, he reports the psychological proceedings: "I admitted that I had watched my professional advancement with considerable interest, and I handsomely added that I yielded to no one in admiration for my private and professional virtues. This was a great point gained. I then endeavoured to work upon my feelings. Conceive my joy when I distinctly perceived a tear glistening in my own eye! Eventually, after a most severe struggle with myself, I reluctantly — most reluctantly — consented" (282). This complicated being embodies British law, and he must confront the embodiment of another law in the Fairy Queen.

The antagonism between the Queen and the Lord Chancellor, the fairies and the peers, has more solid grounds than fantasy. When the fairies menace the peers at the end of Act I and the Queen (wearing a winged Wagnerian helmet in the original production) jabs her spear at the Lord Chancellor, the comic tension is too real to be explained by the incompatibility of mortals and immortals. If *Iolanthe* follows the symbolic implications of *The Wicked World*, the fairies reflect Victorian womanhood; and their conflict with the peers is, in part, a battle of the sexes. "This comes of women interfering in politics," Lord Mountararat complains, after they begin to reform Parliament by assisting Strephon (266).

Gilbert was returning to the conflicts of his early plays, using his burlesque of *The Princess* as the basis of his next opera, *Princess Ida*. *Iolanthe* anticipates the open conflict of the sexes in the Act II finale of *Princess Ida*, where the tensions are expressed in the exciting double chorus as Hildebrand's soldiers burst into the women's college and as the girls' wailing is heard over the aggressive, staccato boasting of men. Masculine condescension rather than aggression provokes the fairies in *Iolanthe*, who become enraged when the peers mistake them for schoolgirls. Their subsequent efforts to remodel Parliament are designed to punish the men for not treating them with enough respect. As in *Princess Ida*, sexual attraction leads finally to reconciliation, but only after the conflict of men and women has added to the tensions between the two worlds of this opera.

At the head of each chorus is a legal purist. The fairy law forbidding marriage with a mortal is sacred to the Fairy Queen, and British law "is the true embodiment/Of everything that's excellent" according to the Lord Chancellor. These antagonists are characterized by recurring musical phrases: the Queen, by the ominous Wagnerian setting of "For a dark sin against our fairy laws"; the Lord Chancellor, by a fugal passage, appropriate to the subtleties of a legal mind.[55] Both laws and their exponents stand in the way of natural impulse. As an Arcadian shepherd, Strephon chafes at the restraints of British law, which prevents him from marrying Phyllis without the Lord Chancellor's consent. (The rivalry of father and son for the same woman recalls the New Comedy of Plautus and Terence, though in this case the men are unaware of their relationship.) The youth resolves to follow "Nature's Acts of Parliament": "When chorused Nature bids me take my love, shall I reply, 'Nay, but a certain Chancellor forbids it'? Sir, you are England's Lord High Chancellor, but are you Chancellor of birds and trees, King of the winds and Prince of thunderclouds?" The Chancellor's reply shows how intent he is upon keeping British law separate from feeling and imagination: Strephon should produce an "affidavit from a thunderstorm, or a few words on oath from a heavy shower." Nothing less would convince the legalist that "chorused Nature has interested herself in the matter" (248).

But feeling has subverted one legalistic mind even before the action begins, and it finally brings together all the persons whom the law would keep apart. The subversion began some twenty years earlier when the Fairy Queen failed to execute Iolanthe for marrying a mortal, and her pardon of Iolanthe in the opening scene marks the triumph of compassion over law. In Act II, when the Queen sees the Guardsman in the sentry box, she becomes fully aware of the conflict between her feelings and her official duties: "If I yielded to a natural impulse, I should fall down and worship that man" (269). Her struggle to "mortify this inclination" parallels the agonizing of the Lord Chancellor as he tries to reconcile marrying Phyllis with his duty as her legal guardian. "I am here in two capacities," he complains, "and they clash, my Lords, they clash!" (277). Neither he nor the Queen is temperamentally suited for keeping an absolute commitment to the letter of the law.

The humane force is embodied in Iolanthe. She gives the opera its lyrical dimension, balancing the satire with a vital romantic theme. As "the life and soul of Fairyland," she has the symbolic role of the anima in romance: she is an emblem of man's creative spirit. Among the fairies she has been their universal artist, with the combined talents of a Gilbert and Sullivan. She wrote their lyrics, composed their music, led their dances, and taught the massive Queen the tricks of a Shakespearean fairy — how to curl inside a buttercup and "swing upon a cobweb" (233). Representing the creative imagination, Iolanthe married a mortal of the most practical mind. As Gilbert's notebook reveals, he was to be a "prosaic person with a horror of fairies & everything supernatural."[56] Iolanthe's choice to defy the law by marrying him generates the subsequent choices that lead to reconciliation. The Queen chooses to pardon her; her son chooses to marry Phyllis, defying mortal law as his mother had defied fairy law. Her example becomes the key to humane behavior by the end of the opera, for it puts freedom and affection above a legalistic respect for fixed codes.

The drama of choice culminates in the second act, which opens with the Sentry meditating upon people's refusals to make choices: they are simply born Liberals or Conservatives. But, from his viewpoint, the world of politics needs stereotyped behavior in order to exist:

> . . . the prospect of a lot
> Of dull M.P.'s in close proximity,
> All thinking for themselves, is what
> No man can face with equanimity.

Lord Mountararat's song, "When Britain really ruled the waves," celebrates the House of Lords for the same reason: the peers have no strength of intellect and hence can do nothing to upset the political life of the country. Then the focus returns to personal decisions, and the Fairy Queen makes a negative choice in suppressing her feelings for the Sentry; Phyllis evades choosing between the two rival peers, who in turn decide not to make a self-sacrifice for the other's benefit; and the peers agree to give up Phyllis altogether. This allows Phyllis and Strephon to decide to marry first and perhaps change their minds afterwards. But the Lord Chancellor now enters the field, having convinced himself of his right to marry Phyllis. His decision sets up the most dramatic choice of all. Fearfully, Iolanthe decides to die rather than allow him to marry their son's chosen bride; she prepares to reveal herself to her husband.

At this moment, the opera moves away from satiric comedy to lyric drama. Sullivan fully realized the action by setting Iolanthe's deliberate revelation of herself against the warning voices of the fairies offstage, whose keening cry has a piognant chromatic descent. In the instant of recognition, the Lord Chancellor ceases to be a buffoon: he embraces Iolanthe with genuine awe and feeling. When the Fairy Queen enters with her company to kill Iolanthe, the keening grows more intense; the fairies move their arms in gestures of ritual mourning until Leila's abrupt "Hold!" breaks the spell and returns the opera to the realm of arbitrary and hence comic decisions.

Since all the fairies have married mortals, the Queen must choose between slaughtering the "whole company" or condoning anarchy. The Lord Chancellor allows her to retain the semblance of legal absolutism by changing the law to make it a capital offence *not* to marry a mortal. Rather than choose the Sentry out of impulse, the Queen must marry him now to avoid the death penalty. But the Chancellor's easy reversal of the law, through "the insertion of a single word," proves the absurdity of her belief that Fairy Law equals Destiny. His solution invites everyone to view legal systems not as absolute powers but as arbitrary creations of men. The Queen had become trapped by a mind-forged manacle, as Frederic and Mabel were by Duty, and as Patience was by her idea that true love is completely unselfish. In its unravelling, the plot of *Iolanthe* dramatizes man's freedom to make choices, to defy laws, and perhaps to send an ancient institution, like the British peerage, off to Fairyland. Yet it also shows that such choices may bring death as close as the Queen's spearpoint.

In the most serious work by Gilbert and Sullivan, *The Yeomen of the Guard,* the characters choose, scheme, and suffer beneath a huge symbol of the law — the Tower of London. With a stern, powerful motif in the overture and in key places in the opera, an image of the Tower dominates the music almost as much as it dominates the stage picture. The Tower motif is a serious counterpart to Sullivan's other evocations of authority: the Wagnerian echoes for the Fairy Queen, the fugal introductions for the Lord Chancellor, and the psuedo-Japanese drumbeats expressing the power of the Mikado.

Under the shadow of the Tower, the action develops as an effort to save an innocent man from execution. The effort is opposed by a sinister set of characters who embody the Tower's authority. These range from the mute headsman to Wilfred Shadbolt, the comic jailor, whose conversation teems with thumbscrews and "anecdotes of the torture chamber." The Tower's most eloquent voice is Dame Hannah, its "housekeeper," who says, "there's not a stone in its

walls that is not as dear to me as my own right hand" (Act, I, II, 141).
For her, the prison means everything that law has meant to the Fairy
Queen: it is as indestructible and unyielding as destiny, "A sentinel
unliving and undying." The Tower signifies both moral and political
law to Dame Hannah, who reads a "legend on its brow" that "tells
of duty done and duty doing."

As an emblem of absolute duty, the Tower is represented by its
Lieutenant, Sir Richard Cholmondeley. He professes abhorrence for
the man whose "scurvy trick" has placed Colonel Fairfax under an
unjust sentence of death: "it is a pity that he should die" (149). Yet
with this feeling, the Lieutenant dutifully prepares to execute the innocent man, and he becomes outraged when Fairfax escapes. His
compassionate officiousness is hardly better than the Mikado's stand
on the letter of the law while sympathizing heartily with its victims:
"Now, let's see about your execution — will after luncheon suit you?
Can you wait till then?" (55).

Fairfax himself does not challenge the Lieutenant's attitude; were
he in charge, he probably would act the same way. He is too stoical
to make a challenge, for to him the Tower is simply a place where he
meets his fate — the "grim old king" — by punctual appointment.
But the Lieutenant's attitude is challenged by Sergeant Meryll, his
son Leonard, and his daughter Phoebe, who arrange for Fairfax to
escape. Phoebe challenges the Tower itself, comparing it to a "cruel
giant in a fairy-tale" (141). As her first song reveals, she is a girl of
quick feelings; and she values her own freedom. But, in plotting to
save Fairfax, she and her father lose personal freedom, she by
promising to marry the jailor, and he by proposing to Dame Hannah.
Being pragmatists, they may find a way out; but, to some degree,
free action and defiance of the law lead them into a trap, shadowed
by the stern Tower.

The trap closes tightest on the focal character, Jack Point. As
strolling players, he and Elsie Maynard move freely until they accept
the Lieutenant's proposal that she marry Fairfax before his execution. Elsie's loss of freedom through this marriage gives her just what
she chooses in the second act — a handsome, noble husband. Thinking that her unknown husband has been shot, she consents to marry
Fairfax, who courts her while disguised as Leonard Meryll.
Ironically, it was Jack Point's idea to report the death of her husband; and this report allowed her to choose a romantic lover instead
of himself. This second reversal of his schemes destroys his power of
action; for unlike Phoebe, he has no resilience: she can give way to

tears and vent her resentment against Fairfax — "this is his gratitude!" (192) — and still retain enough spirit to plot once more to save him, and she can rejoice at his reprieve. But Jack Point completely reverses roles, dropping the comic mask and exposing miserable self-pity. His verse in the quartet expresses a total sense of defeat:

> When a jester
> Is outwitted,
> Feelings fester,
> Heart is lead!
> Food for fishes
> Only fitted,
> Jester wishes
> He was dead!
> (192)

The comedy has ended for him, just as it would for the clowns in *Pagliacci*, produced four years after *The Yeomen* in 1892. All he can do now is evoke pity, and pity is what he begs for in the last scene — after a career of soliciting laughter. Whether interpreted as death or fainting, his falling "insensible" at the end represents the collapse of his spirit. The jester's mask cannot fit the shape of his grief over losing Elsie.

When he falls, the Tower stands in the background, looming over the one character who is destroyed by the events arising from an unjust imprisonment. The opera ends with ironic contrasts: instead of a public execution, the climactic scene is a wedding celebration, interrupted by a frail jester; the bride and groom embrace as he falls at their feet. The players' folk melody is sung once more before the awesome prison, and the "singing farce of the Merryman and his Maid" — which had told of an imagined reunion — now tells of their separation. If there is a secret source for these ironies, it should lie hidden somewhere in the recesses of the Tower. Gilbert made the Tower his most emphatic symbol of something larger than British or Fairy law and something beyond human power to outwit, alter, or fully understand. Its dark presence gives *The Yeomen of the Guard* a final undertone of tragedy.

III.   Tensions within the Partnership and the Operas of the 1890's

With *The Yeomen*, Gilbert went the farthest he dared in the direction of serious opera. Though it ran for over four hundred nights, he seemed to feel that the public had no taste for any more sober light operas by himself and Sullivan. He was, of course, unable to forecast the popularity of this work when it was revived a few years later.[57] Sullivan, too, was disappointed over the alleged "indifference of the public" to his most ambitious opera, but his satisfaction with the music and with the reviewers' praise strengthened his urge to set texts of a "more serious and romantic character."[58] For over two decades people had been telling him that his talents were for greater things than comic opera. While still in his teens, he had composed the music for *The Tempest* which made him famous upon his return from Leipzig; and in his early twenties he had written a romantic symphony with a first movement of special vitality and promise. The recording of this work — over a century after its first performance — helps to explain why Victorian critics chided him for turning out so many drawing-room ballads and comic operas.[59]

After *The Mikado,* Sullivan regained his reputation in oratorio with *The Golden Legend* (1886); and in the operas of this decade — especially in the two songs for Princess Ida, the ghost scene in *Ruddigore,* and the funeral march from *The Yeomen* — there were moments when he filled the Savoy with music of serious dimensions. Now, after the production of *The Yeomen,* Richard D'Oyly Carte was offering him the chance to write grand opera for the new Royal English Opera House.[60] Sullivan asked Gilbert for a libretto; but, though Gilbert claimed that a "consistent subject" was "far more congenial to my taste than the burlesque of *Iolanthe* or *The Mikado,*" he rejected the invitation to venture into serious drama: "we should be risking everything. . . ."[61]

His caution was heightened not only by the moderate success of *The Yeomen* but by the downright failure in the same year of his melodrama, *Brantinghame Hall.* He had received no critical encouragement to return to the serious mode of *Gretchen* and *Broken Hearts.* But Sullivan insisted that there could be no retreat from their achievement in their latest work. If its failure to equal the popular success of *The Mikado* "means a return to our former style of piece, I must say at once, with deep regret, that I cannot do it. I have lost the liking for comic opera."[62] He wanted to do a work "where the music is to be the first consideration — where words are to suggest music, not govern it, and where music will intensify and emphasize the emotional effect of the words."[63]

Gilberts's response was exasperation at Sullivan's idea that he had been "effacing" himself in their partnership: "If we meet, it must be as master and master. . . ."[64] After they did come to terms in May,

1889, Gilbert offered what in some ways was a compromise and what in other ways was an evasion of Sullivan's demands. He had already suggested the simplest part of the compromise: if Sullivan wanted to write grand opera, why not do so with another librettist, while setting a new comic opera by Gilbert? Sullivan finally accepted this arrangement, which was rather like betting on two horses in the same race; and the results were his and Gilbert's *The Gondoliers* in December, 1889, and his serious *Ivanhoe*, with words by Julian Sturgis, which opened auspiciously in January, 1891 but later failed to win a place in the repertoire of even an English opera company, though it was revived briefly by Sir Thomas Beecham in 1910. Gilbert's second part in the compromise is reflected in the long verse passage at the start of *The Gondoliers*, for it gave Sullivan a chance to work on "a larger musical scale" without facing interruptions of dialogue. The second act also thrust responsibility upon him, with its unusually elaborate finale and its call for two dances, the cachucha and the gavotte, where the orchestra is heard at length without Gilbert's words.

After the "carpet quarrel" and the failure of either artist to win a smashing success with another partner, Gilbert and Sullivan returned to the pattern of *The Gondoliers* for their last two operas. There are second-act dances in both *Utopia* and *The Grand Duke*, with music written independently of words. Gilbert wrote long first-act finales and supplied an unusual number of ensemble pieces — two successive quintets in Act I of *The Grand Duke;* a duet followed by two trios in Act II of *Utopia.* In both works, a tendency appears to double or even triple the stock elements of the earlier operas. There are three processional entrances in the first act of *Utopia;* there are two mock-melodramatic numbers for Julia Jellicoe in *The Grand Duke*, plus a highly operatic recitative and song. After the leading roles had been doubled in *The Gondoliers*, these last operas continued to call for larger casts and longer time for performance.

But the extra length is not simply the result of letting Sullivan write more music. The dialogue has long stretches also — as if Gilbert were determined to gain equal time with the composer. The wordiness of the last libretti is a partial evasion of Sullivan's demand, for the proportion of dialogue to verse has not been significantly reduced, and Sullivan might still have complained that the operas were "Gilbert's pieces with music added by me."[65] But the clearest evasion appears in the tone of these works; for rather than moving toward romantic seriousness, they are almost emotionless, with far less dramatic tension than *H. M. S. Pinafore* and with no moments of pathos like those in *Iolanthe*. In tone, they could hardly be more remote from *The Yeomen of the Guard*. Perhaps Sullivan's disappointment over *Ivanhoe* made him less insistent upon a piece with serious emotion. The feelings that Gilbert encouraged him to express were the joy and abandon of the cachucha and the Offenbachian license of a comedian's sham court in *The Grand Duke*. But freedom to compose dance music was not what Sullivan had pled for in 1889.

The verdict of the public on the last operas of Gilbert and Sullivan was discouraging, and the D'Oyly Carte Opera Company has never ventured a revival of either *Utopia* or *The Grand Duke*. Two of Gilbert's non-Sullivan operas from his late period have perhaps been deservedly forgotten, though *His Excellency* (1894) has a couple of witty songs and a little distinction as a musical farce. *The Fallen Fairies* (1909) is *The Wicked World* in opera form, for long segments of dialogue were lifted from the play Gilbert had written thirty-six years earlier. Having an all-women chorus, it lacks the musical and dramatic possibilities of his best libretti. But the neglect of his three main operas of the 1890's may be less justified. The fact that *The Mountebacks* (1892), *Utopia Limited* (1893), and *The Grand Duke*(1896) achieved only moderate runs does not in itself prove that they are inferior works of art. *Ruddigore* and *Princess Ida* ran little longer than *Utopia;* and the D'Oyly Carte Opera Company did not revive them until after World War I; but they reflect the fullest talents of their authors, who ranked them among their best works. Few critics would argue that *H. M. S. Pinafore* is twice as good as *Ruddigore* simply because it ran twice as long, for Victorian taste was not infallible. "What people want now is simple 'fun', and little else," D'Oyly Carte wrote to Gilbert, after *Utopia* had begun to wane. If Carte was right, the short runs of these operas may reflect more upon the frivolity of the audience of this era than upon any weakness in the words or music.

On the other hand, while people crowded to the Gaiety Theatre to see the newest musical comedy, there were still large numbers returning to the Savoy for revivals of *The Mikado* and *Pinafore*. And the hardly frivolous *Yeomen of the Guard* ran for six months in 1897.[66] These facts make it difficult to accuse the public of a decadent lapse in taste. A partisan for Gilbert could blame the failures on his composers, whose health, if not talents, were certainly in decline: Alfred Cellier died before the opening of *The Mountebanks*, and Sullivan became deathly ill early in 1892. Cellier's choral passages sound thin in comparison with Sullivan's harmonies, and much of the score for *The Mountebanks* lacks the master's humor and vivacity. But the only complete recording of this opera reveals that some numbers, like the ticking clockwork trio in Act II, rival Sullivan at his most ingenious, and the other music has more than historical interest.[67]

As for *Utopia* and *The Grand Duke*, Sullivan's contribution has been severely criticized,[68] usually by men who have never heard a professional performance of either work. Listeners at the Savoy were more favorably impressed. Bernard Shaw praised the score of *Utopia*,[69] and Gilbert told Sullivan that his setting of the Act I finale was the best in the whole series.[70] First-night reviewers of *The Grand Duke* tended to speak well of the music: "Sullivan is splended," *Fun* reported;[71] but the *Graphic* noted that two of his most brilliant numbers — the parody of the "vulgar chansonette of the Parisian music hall" and the Grecian chorus — were "a little above the heads of the audience."[72] Even in amateur recordings, the music sounds less feeble than critics have claimed; and there are moments in "Strange the views," the mock-duel between Ludwig and Rudolph, the opening of Act II, and the Roulette Song when the listener can almost understand why the music was once called "Sullivan at his best."[73]

In fairness to Gilbert's partners and his public, much of the blame for the unpopularity of these operas probably rests on his shoulders. His beloved "lozenge plot" unfolds mechanically in the second act of *The Mountebanks*, when a succession of scenes demonstrates the effects of the magic potion on various sets of characters. The resolution is not achieved by Gilbertian logic, as in *The Mikado* and *Ruddigore*,[74] or even by a burlesque recognition scene, as in *Pinafore* and *The Gondoliers*. Instead, a jealous woman has a sudden change of heart after "*struggling with her better feelings,*" and she restores the talisman that saves everyone from the magic spell. Not only is her response counter to what Gilbert reveals of her character, but it tends to take the sting out of all the jibes at human selfishness that have come before. His two libretti for Sullivan are also weakened in key places by windy dialogue: a long exposition scene gets *Utopia* off to a slow start, and four pages of prosing over Rudolph's miserliness prolong the first-act marathon of *The Grand Duke*. Compared with the earlier Savoy operas, the last two are massive and sprawling; their plots are looser and less purposeful; they run greater risks of boring the audience.

But, in spite of these drawbacks, these works are significant expressions of Gilbert's chief satiric themes. In *The Mountebanks*, his basic complaint against human nature is written on the label of the magic potion; and it is dramatized by the transformations that follow: "*Man is a hypocrite, and invariably affects to be better than he really is.*" The magic punishes the characters by making them "*exactly what they pretend to be.*" The satire upon playing roles is enforced by the mountebank's life-sized clockwork dolls — "chock full of eccentric wheels," Bartolo reports, " — might almost be English." After depicting stereotyped behavior for over two decades, Gilbert at last brings an emblem of it onstage; and he uses the dolls to create a scene of elemental satiric force. Transformed into a mechanical Hamlet and Ophelia, Bartolo and Nina enter stiffly in Act II, wearing placards that say "*Put a penny in the slot.*" Their duet affirms what Hesketh Pearson has called Gilbert's "irradicable faith in the corruptibility of all mankind":[75]

BAR.   If our action's stiff and crude,
          Do not laugh because it's rude.
NI.   If our gestures promise larks,
          Do not make unkind remarks.
BAR.   Clockwork figures may be found
          Everywhere and all around.
NI.   Ten to one, if we but knew,
          You are clockwork figures too.
BAR.   And the motto of the lot,
NI.   "Put a penny in the slot!"

With the placards, the simple melody by Cellier, and the taunting address to the audience, the scene has a stark directness more like Brecht and Weill's *Three-Penny Opera* than anything in Gilbert and Sullivan. It illustrates Franz Kafka's belief that by exaggeration a situation might become "perfectly clear."[76]

Gilbert's next opera is another extreme formulation of ideas that had haunted him since *The Happy Land* and *Topsy-Turvydom.* As a timely vehicle for his vision of political absurdity, he took up the utopian motif that had become prominent through Edward Bellamy's *Looking Backward* (1888) and the responses of such British socialists as William Morris in *News from Nowhere* (1890) and George Bernard Shaw, Sidney and Beatrice Webb, and other members of the Fabian Society. With the punning title, *Utopia (Limited)*, Gilbert introduced a capitalist contradiction into the stream of socialist thought: his utopia becomes a joint-stock company. At the same time, "Limited" expresses the usual Gilbertian skepticism concerning human efforts to construct any system of absolute value. More directly than *Iolanthe* itself, *Utopia* works out the formula in his *Iolanthe* Notebook;

The piece should show the miseries of a millenium:

All party strife
All war
All legal dissension   } abolished
All religious differences
All disease

consequently —

All patriots
All soldiers and sailors
All barristers   } are thrown out of work.[77]
All clergymen
All doctors

The plot develops the ironies of this Mandevillian idea. One is the Utopians' assurance that being perfect means being English. As Gilbert wrote in the notebook for this opera, they are "confirmed Anglo-maniacs,"[78] who admire British prudery ("How English and how pure!"); English artists (a native tenor calls himself Mr. Wilkinson); English fashions; and, above all, English political institutions. They can even sing jubilantly about the Joint-Stock Companies Act of 1862, which Gilbert attacks for protecting unethical speculators from bankruptcy. In Act II, when King Paramount reports the "thorough Anglicizing" of Utopia, every comparison with England is ironic. The six "Flowers of Progress" from the model country either lie brazenly — "We haven't any slummeries in England" — or speak with the wildest optimism:

KING   We have solved the labour question with discrimination
       polished,
     So poverty is obsolete and hunger is abolished —

FLOWERS OF PROGRESS We are going to abolish it in England.

                   (V. II, 330)

Topical allusions heighten the irony of letting England represent perfection. When Captain Corcoran enters during the first-act finale and sings "We never run a ship ashore," the subsequent "hardly ever" could have reminded Gilbert's audience of at least three recent naval disasters. Sheer delight in a quotation from *Pinafore*, or puzzlement over this captain's identity (was he the original captain or the former Ralph Rackstraw?) might have blunted the point of the allusion, but Gilbert was glancing at a painful reality. In 1891, the iron-clad man-of-war, *Anson*, had collided with a passenger ship named the *Utopia;* over five hundred lives were lost.[79] A second disaster led to the court martial of a vice-admiral after the *Howe* ran aground in November, 1892.[80] In the summer before the first performance of *Utopia*, the most embarrassing of these calamities had occurred when the *Camperdown* and the *Victoria* had collided on a naval maneuver, killing over three hundred and twenty men.[81] Captain Corcoran's boast was a reminder of how much there was to learn in the navigation of unwieldy — and quickly sinking — iron ships.

In a less painful allusion, Lady Sophy's anxieties about the King's sexual mores invited the audience to smile at their own future king whose conduct had provoked scandalous rumours since the 1860's.[82] The Prince of Wales' only complaint about *Utopia*, however, was that King Paramount wore the Order of the Garter on the uniform of a Field Marshal and that he alone in England "was entitled to this double distinction."[83] Gilbert wrote to Sullivan that no one had complained because some of the peers in *Iolanthe* wore the Garter, but he suggested that it be removed since "the Field-Marshal's Uniform makes it rather more personal to H. R. H."

But the central irony of *Utopia* goes beyond topical satire. According to Gilbert's formula, complete reform disrupts society by leaving its guardians — soldiers, clergymen, lawyers, doctors — with nothing to do. The Utopians rebel against the perfect society, as if to demonstrate the idea that most men are too corrupt to want a millennium, even if one were possible. Zara has to placate them by introducing government by party, the institution which will undo all the reforms. Gilbert does not offer this resolution in the spirit of a Mandeville who argues that private vices create public good, for Zara's last speech contains some of Gilbert's bitterest lines in which he chides the nation for not having achieved far greater social reform than it had by 1893. Quoted here from the first-night version, Zara's praise of government by party is an ironic censure of English politics

and an unhappy resignation to the rule of muddle: "Introduce that
great and glorious element — at once the bulwark and foundation of
England's greatness — and all will be well! No political measures
will endure, because one Party will assuredly undo all that the other
Party has done . . . no social reform will be attempted, because out of
vice, squalor, and drunkenness no political capital is to be
made. . . ."[84]

After these ironies, the cocky strains of "Rule Britannia" sound
blatantly out of place, and the words to the revised finale express the
doubts about the well-being and the future of Great Britain that the
opera had already raised. In retrospect, after the world wars or even
the Boer War, the ending seems to verge on prophecy. King
Paramount sings naïvely of how England "holds the peace of Europe
in her hand/With half a score invincible battalions," but the chorus
voices a suspicion of the contrast between rumor and reality:

> Such, at least, is the tale
> Which is borne on the gale,
>   From the island which dwells in the sea.
> Let us hope, for her sake,
> That she makes no mistake —
>   That she's all she professes to be!

The words approach doggerel, but their message needed to be
heard in a decade of imperial self-importance. Perhaps this criticism
was one reason for the public's refusal to give the opera a lengthy
run.

Compared with *Utopia Limited, The Grand Duke* looks like a
retreat from satire. Aside from its eighteenth-century setting, it
suggests an effort to produce the "modern farcical comedy set to
music" that D'Oyly Carte had requested. But Gilbert's eighteenth
century contains dynamite, and his "ugly misshapen little brat"[85]
has undertones of timely satiric force. Its motifs are ugly: compulsive
role-playing, avarice, and ambition are matched with images of
nausea ("this feeling of warm oil"), biliousness, and general
decrepitude. Duke Rudolph's song, "When you find you're a
brokendown critter," captures the quite literal decadence of this
1890's opera. Rudolph is the feeble emblem of authority, the dying
"old king" in the comic ritual. His chamberlains insult him behind
his back, and his subjects plot revolution. Like King Paramount in
Utopia and many European monarchs at this time, he lives in fear of
death by dynamite ("it mixes one up awfully").[86] Instead of being

assassinated, however, he submits to "legal death" in a Statutory Duel, losing by design to Ludwig, the comedian who replaces him as a "lord of misrule."[87] Chaos ensues, as Ludwig finds himself married to two women and engaged to two more; he leads the actors in drinking bouts and reckless dancing; and his Ducal Palace momentarily becomes a casino rivaling Monte Carlo. The action is largely the dissolution of an order which never appears worth saving.

Amidst the sickness, drunkenness, and gambling, the decadence of *The Grand Duke* is also sustained by allusions to Shakespeare's cynical drama of political and social corruption, *Troilus and Cressida*; for the actors appear in costume for their roles in *Troilus and Cressida* throughout the second act. In both works, dishonesty and opportunism disrupt private and public life; and the opera achieves a dimension of political satire by dramatizing an analogy between the theater and politics. An equation is set up by Ernest's first song: "the man who can rule a theatrical crew . . . Can govern this tuppenny State!" (361). The ducal court is run like a theater, with Rudolph planning his wedding as if it were a stage play. The second royal court has its own costumier who dresses and rehearses the vulgar noblemen attending the Prince of Monte Carlo. These "wealthy members of the brewing interest" have become both peers and "supernumeraries" (416 - 17). On the other side of the equation, the real actors become political conspirators, and they struggle among themselves for power with the skill and pettiness of experienced courtiers. The comedian Ludwig makes the shrewdest political move of all when he revives the provision for Statutory Duels — the combat by drawing cards which inflicts legal nonexistence upon the loser.

The falseness of both the political and theatrical worlds is implied by the construction of *The Grand Duke*. It is put together like a series of minute plays within a play: real actors play at being actors, who in turn play at dueling, at reviving Athenian glory, and at ruling a grand duchy. At times the emphasis on costume and ceremony suggests an elaborate game of charades, especially in Act II when Ludwig tries to guess the identity of the Prince of Monte Carlo. Twice the leading lady, Julia Jellicoe, demonstrates how she would act the part of the Grand Duke's bride — first, by stressing the domesticity of a sentimental heroine; second, by feigning the jealousy, rage, and madness of a *femme fatale*. Two Statutory Duels are fought in the first act; the second mock combat opens the finale with simulated fury after the Duke agrees with Ludwig to accept twenty-four hours of legal death. Hurling abuse at each other, the combatants stage a scene resembling a genuine *agon* in Aristophanes.

More directly than in any of the other operas, Gilbert invites the audience to notice the theatrical pretenses. He sends Ludwig forward in Grecian costume to confide in the audience near the start of Act II, achieving the effect of a *parabasis* in Aristophanes; but, instead of boasting of the play's excellence, Ludwig admits the pretentiousness of the academic wit in his comic song:

> *[Confidentially to audience]*
> At this juncture I may mention
> That this erudition sham
> Is but classical pretension,
> The result of steady "cram." . . .
>   (398)

This song implicates even the librettist in his picture of political and theatrical falsity, and the satire of the theater makes *The Grand Duke* a recapitulation of Gilbert's parody plays and his operatic burlesques in the 1860's. At the same time, it reflects his later experience as a stage director and author who often clashed with actors and with his own collaborator. His difficulties with "a theatrical crew" had been increased by the tension with Sullivan and D'Oyly Carte following the "carpet quarrel"; and the power struggle with these men at the Savoy was enough to show him how professional rivalries could disrupt personal relationships.

Partly because they are such professionals, his characters in *The Grand Duke* are studies in how not to relate to other people. Professional duties, not personal ones, are the absolute laws of their world. A too-confident notary presides over the action, pronouncing the judgment which all the actors repeat with enthusiasm:

> Though marriage contracts — or whate'er you call 'em —
> Are very solemn,
> Dramatic contracts (which you all adore so)
> Are even more so!
>   (394)

A "legal ghoest" [sic.] haunts a world where personal feelings count for nothing and official roles are everything. In this comic nightmare, laws are more real than life, and men who suffer "social death" in a duel with cards are treated as if they have no identity. The nightmare lurks in Julia Jellicoe's insistence that "legal technicalities cannot be defied" (412); the comedy comes from believing that she is wrong. No one in *The Grand Duke* has the intelligence to assert his own freedom, as Alice does in Wonderland, and to see the legal deadlock as the result of an arbitrary game in which people let their lives be ruled by a pack of cards. Even Ludwig, the most active schemer, becomes a patient victim of legalistic process. After winning the throne, he immediately forfeits his power by accepting Julia's claim to be his rightful bride, and in the tipsy second act he lets himself be passed from one woman to the next as the Baroness and the Princess of Monte Carlo each come to claim possession. Everyone stays under the power of the law until the end, and they escape only through luck. The legal expert was wrong: the ace counts as the lowest card in a Statutory Duel, making Ludwig's victories illegal. Had he drawn the right card, the confusion in Phennig-Halbphennig would have lasted until someone realized that personal identity is more than a matter of roles, rules, and social definitions. Only then could "legal technicalities" be defied.

CHAPTER 4

The Individual and the Law

I N Gilbert's last play, a one-act "Character Study" called *The Hooligan* (1911), the law confronts the individual with the force of a nightmare. The scene is a prison cell on the day set for the execution of Nat Solly, "a hooligan lad of twenty," who has been condemned to die for the murder of his sweetheart. The action comes from his desperate effort to be free. But each night he dreams of guilt and bondage in an enormous courtroom,

half a mile acrost an' a quarter of a mile deep, wiv a red judge ever so far off in the middle; five 'undred jurymen on one side, a couple of 'undred lawyers in the middle, an' a thousand public coves on the other, the jury noddin' *their* 'eds all the time and the lawyers noddin' their 'eds, an' the public noddin' theirs — all a-noddin' 'cept the hol' judge. An' 'e says, says 'e, "Prisoner at the bar," says 'e, "them jurymen has found you guilty; and blow me if I ain't o' their way of thinkin'," says 'e, "and this 'ere's the sentence," says 'e, an' 'e, claps a black cap on 'is nopper, an' 'is two arms stretches out o' his red togs, an' they grows longer an' longer — quarter o' a mile long they grows — till 'is fists is close to my froat, the bilin' in court noddin' their heads all the time, as much as to say, "That's right; go on; give it 'im." An' when 'e reaches me 'e clutches me round the gullet and squeedges me wiv both 'ands till I am fair choked, the crowd a-noddin' all the time, as if to say, "Just so; we quite agrees; go on." An' just when I feels I'm a-dyin', I gives a screech and wakes up shiverin' wiv cold an' all of a 'ot perspiration, like a bloomin' toad, wiv my 'art a'beatin' nineteen to the dozen.[1]

With the nodding unanimity of the court, the dream foreshadows the scene from Kafka's *Trial*, where, in a room filled with fog and a great crowd, Joseph K — discovers that everyone but himself wears the same badge, including the examining Magistrate. Unlike Joseph K — , Solly wakes up from his nightmare, but he feels nothing of Alice's triumph over a pack of cards in Wonderland. Solly awakens to the walls of his cell and his consuming fear of death.

His fear is the source of the drama in this brief play, for he will not accept death. Until the last hour before his execution, he keeps looking for a reprieve in answer to his petition. Sobbing because there is no answer, he has none of the stoicism of Colonel Fairfax in *The Yeomen*. Solly's fight against death becomes a drama with a central irony, as the conflict within his mind emerges in his nightmare and in his tireless defenses against guilt. Though he has killed his sweetheart, he insists that the law should not apply to him: "I ain't like a' ordinary bloke. I'm feeble-minded; the doctor said so, and 'e'd know. Then I've never 'ad no chanct, I've never been taught nuffin, and I've got a weak 'art. I was in the 'orsepital six weeks wiv a weak 'art. Oh, my Gawd! it's 'ard! it's 'ard! . . . Am I to be judged like a bloke wot's been brought up fair and strite, and taught a tride, and can look on a ticker wiv 'is hooks safe in 'is trousers pockets?" (98). With this reversal of the superman theory, Solly puts himself outside (or below) the law. Gilbert's respect for the argument is suggested by his own behavior as a justice of the peace who would not face a prisoner without asking himself, "What chance in life has this man had?"[2] His viewpoint was expressed years earlier in Strephon's omitted song from *Iolanthe:*

> Take a wretched thief
> Through the City sneaking,
> Pocket handkerchief
> Ever, ever sneaking:
> What is he but I
> Robbed of all my chances —
> Picking pockets by
> Force of circumstances?
> I might have been as bad —
> As unlucky, rather —
> If I'd only had
> Fagin for a father![3]

But Solly's effort to win sympathy involves desperate rationalizations. He insists that he had only meant to wound his girl friend, but "my 'and slipped (I never 'ad no luck) and I cut deeper than I meant." Later he explains that his hand slipped "on account of youth and inexperience." With these arguments for excuses, he tries to see himself as the forgiving victim of official ignorance: "*(Furiously)* 'Devil strike me blind, but if I 'ad that blarsted old howl of a judge 'ere — that cussed old turnip- 'ed wiv a wig on it, — I'd' *(checking himself with an effort)* 'I'd forgive 'im. S'elp me I'd forgive 'im. . . . Strike 'em all blind, I'd forgive the 'ole bleedin' lot' " (100).

Self-justification ends when the cell door opens and Solly imagines that his executioners have come. He makes a frantic confession of guilt, hoping for extra time with the chaplain; then he damns everyone and fights to escape. The ironies of the drama now became apparent, for the Governor of the Prison announces that the death sentence has been reduced to life-imprisonment. Solly's arguments about his unlucky past — even his "youth and inexperience" — have swayed the Judge and the Home Secretary; his "fearful doom" has apparently been averted. At this moment, the "faint-hearted" young man springs up, gives a cry of pain, and falls to the floor. A doctor pronounces him dead of heart failure. He has escaped from the sort of law which entangles so many Gilbertian characters, only to succumb to the law which no man — not even a Lord Chancellor — can alter.

Within its narrow limits, *The Hooligan* is a vital dramatization of the conflict between the individual and the law. Solly's desperation, if nothing else, wins him sympathy in his fight for life. But, like Gilbert's other serious plays, *The Hooligan* is a nearly forgotten work. The free actions of Mrs. Theobald in *Ought We to Visit Her?*, of the Lady Hilda in *Broken Hearts*, of Mrs. Van Brugh in *Charity* had no power to survive in the public mind. In comic contexts, the heroine's choice to sacrifice herself for her son in *Iolanthe* and Sir Ruthven's decision to defy the curse in *Ruddigore* illustrate the kinds of dramatic action that the serious works represent. The drama of choice demanded seriousness, for choices are more risky in Gilbert's worlds than unthinking conformity. To live freely, Mrs. Theobald gives up trying for a place in society; in a worse situation, Galatea gives up her life in order to restore peace to her master's household.

In depicting such characters, Gilbert himself ran the risk of seeming like a conformist who merely imitated the countless renunciatory heroines of Victorian melodrama and fiction. For serious drama, the choice needed to appear as the plausible act of an individualized character; but Gilbert was unsuited for creating realistic characters in two ways. First, his talent in drawing and writing was for stylization: he perceived types more clearly than individuals. Second, his comic view of a world where anything can happen — where characters like Grosvenor in *Patience* and the Reverend Hopley Porter suddenly reverse roles — contrasts with the vision of stern causality in tragic and naturalistic art. Gilbert could prescribe a way to maintain identity in a song — "Be nobody else but you," — as Mr. Goldberg tells the princesses in *Utopia*, but to represent the struggle for identity in drama that would seem convincing after Ibsen's plays was beyond his power.

Gilbert's success lay in comically exposing compulsive behavior. Through exaggeration and fantasy, he revealed the human penchant for acting like machines. The characters in *Creatures of Impulse* jerk about like tightly wound toys; the Duke, the Colonel, and the Major become esthetic marionettes in *Patience;* Bartolo and Nina become clockwork dolls in *The Mountebanks.* These images bring into focus Gilbert's sense that people seek conformity rather than the responsibilities of free decision; it is this world, and not Utopia, where "our political opinions are formed for us by the journals to which we subscribe" (282).

In satirizing the mechanical aspects of political and social life, Gilbert focuses upon convention and ceremony. Exaggeration marks his satire of convention: one of the most vivid examples is "Etiquette," the Bab ballad in which two ship-wrecked Englishmen deprive themselves of good food and fellowship because each knows the other's disreputable friend. Through parody Gilbert attacked the habits of moral perception that were encouraged by melodrama: *A Sensation Novel* and *Engaged* upset the conventional equation of good looks and success with virtue. Ceremony underlies the structure of his operas, giving them some of the ritualistic appeal of the comedies of Aristophanes. But, at the same time, ceremony reflects the officiousness and pomp of late Victorian life. Being punctilious himself, Gilbert was ideally suited to mimic the fussiness of a King Edward who "chastized his grandson for wearing the uniform of one regiment of Foot Guards with the spurs of another."[4] The last operas contain the most vivid parodies of ritualized behavior: the royal drawing room in *Utopia*, with King Paramount dressed so precisely like the Prince of Wales that the Prince objected; and the entrance of Duke Rudolph with his seven chamberlains, who pass along a royal handkerchief in time to Sullivan's unhurried music, while Rudolph fights back a grand ducal sneeze. ("It's stately and impressive," he confides to the audience, "and it's really very cheap.")

Despite the generations of enthusiasm for the Savoy operas, the significance of Gilbert's achievement has often been questioned. He himself called the operas "twaddle."[5] *The Gondoliers* was a piece of "ridiculous rubbish,"[6] and he said that his estate at Grim's Dyke represented "the folly of the British Public."[7] The complete sincerity of these judgments can be doubted, partly because Gilbert was smarting over the neglect of his serious work when he made them, and partly because his actions belie his words: to the time of his death, he was intent on seeing that the operas were tastefully revived.

More specific and probably more sincere criticism came from the man who succeeded Gilbert as Britain's major comic dramatist. George Bernard Shaw objected that Gilbert did not take his paradoxes seriously. Thinking of such proto-Shavian lines as the Pirate King's remark about respectability, Shaw complained that Gilbert "would put forward a paradox which at first promised to be one of those humane truths which so many modern men of fine spiritual insight, from William Blake onward, have worded so as to flash out their contradiction of some weighty rule of our systematized morality, and would then let it slip through his fingers, leaving nothing but a mechanical topsy-turvitude."[8] Shaw tried to illustrate this failing by contrasting *The Pirates of Penzance* with *The Wild Duck* (1884): the theme of both "is essentially the same"; but, where Gilbert turns slavery to duty into a joke, Ibsen makes "a grimly serious attack on our notion that we need stick at nothing in the cause of duty."[9]

In defense of Gilbert, the simplest thing to say is that he makes a comic, not a "grimly serious," attack on compulsive moral idealism. An attack can be both comic and satiric, and Shaw should have realized that Gilbert invites the audience to question duty as a rule of life, once it has been divorced from personal feeling, religious belief, and charity. Mabel and Frederic in *The Pirates* appear ridiculous in their slavery to this detached abstraction; Gregers Werle in *The Wild Duck* becomes horrible; but in both cases the value of rigid idealism is called into question. Rather than defining Gilbert's limitations, Shaw revealed an attitude that sometimes weakens his own comic art — the undercurrent of preachiness that surfaces at the end of *Major Barbara* and makes his enthusiasm for an idea — Bergson's *élan vital* — seem naïvely uncritical in *Man and Superman*. When Shaw contrasted his first popular comedy with *Engaged*, he exposed a self-important belief in his powers of uplifting the audience — not through comedy but "philosophy": "It is the positive element in my philosophy that makes *Arms and the Man* a perfectly genuine play about real people, with a happy ending and hope and life in it, instead of a thing like *Engaged.* . . ."[10]

Shaw considered Gilbertian irony "barren cynicism." By contrast
with *Engaged*, where each character has a perverse viewpoint, *Arms
and the Man* is quite straightforward, and the hero states the
"positive" philosophy so directly that the author himself seems to
come on stage: "now that youve found that life isnt a farce, but
something quite sensible and serious, what further obstacle is there
to your happiness?"[11] Not only did Shaw distrust Gilbert's irony: in
one of his prefaces he sounded distrustful of laughter itself. A strange
attitude for a comic dramatist, it fits easily with Shaw's complaint
that Gilbert failed to take his parodoxes seriously. In "real life,"
Shaw wrote, "we laugh and exult in destruction, confusion, and ruin.
When a comedy is performed, it is nothing to me that the spectators
laugh: any fool can make an audience laugh. I want to see how many
of them, laughing or grave, are in the melting mood."[12] Had Gilbert
held so dismal a view of laughter, he might not have carried irony as
far as he does in *Engaged* and in *The Pirates*. But he had a different
vision, and Jack Point's assertion in *The Yeomen of the Guard*
probably springs from it: "look you, there is humor in all things, and
the truest philosophy is that which teaches us to find it and make the
most of it."

That philosophy may be less searching and avant-garde than
Shaw's seemed to be at the turn of the century, and it proves unequal to Jack Point's later experience, but such a view at least allows
for a comprehensive comic vision. Unburdened by a constructive
program, Gilbert could indulge in parody and satiric ridicule without
pausing to explain or defend a "positive" social or economic theory.
Anyone who wanted to know his values could find them stated
clearly at the end of *Charity* (he did not invent them) and could
realize that honesty and a charitable concern for others were the
values implied by the ironies of his comic works. As a satirist without
a program, Gilbert may have achieved some of Shaw's own social-
political ends, perhaps with equal effect. In a hyperbolic essay
published soon after World War I, one writer asserted that in spite of
his apparent conservatism, Gilbert "did more to cut away the props
of the old world, to prepare the minds of the unthinking mass for
change, than any who deliberately preached against the established
order. If Gilbert had been a professed revolutionary, he would have
had as little influence as Bernard Shaw. . . . Because people laughed
with him, they fancied he was one of themselves and let him under-
mine their faith in much that they held sacred."[13]

The claim is exaggerated, but the grain of truth in it may have been evidenced by the renewed popularity in the 1920's of Gilbert and Sullivan in London and New York. With their unforgettable tunes, Gilbert's lines entered the public memory and reminded a new generation of the proven flaws and the weighty self-importance of governmental institutions. As the essayist pointed out in 1921, the satire in the Major-General's Song in *The Pirates* was made sadly relevant by the blunders of generals in the Boer War and World War I. Perhaps also Sir Joseph's success story and the vision of Parliament in *Iolanthe* worked, in some way, "to create that distrust of politicians which has been going ever since." Other forces than comic operas no doubt had some influence, but one point can be accepted without reservation: Gilbert's satire "sank into the mind of his age."[14] Animated by Sullivan's music, *The Mikado, Pinafore, The Pirates, Iolanthe,* and *The Gondoliers* have stayed alive, both on the stage and in the imagination. "I was present at a rehearsal of the first Act of an undiscovered Gilbert and Sullivan opera, last night, in my dreams," Rupert Brooke wrote to Virginia Stephen in 1912, "But I have forgotten the tunes."[15] What more could Gilbert achieve? Even his unwritten works pursue the mind into its fantasies.

Notes and References

Chapter One

1. "An Autobiography," *Theatre*, N.S., I (April 2, 1883), 217.
2. "Johnny Pounce,"*Foggerty's Fairy and Other Tales* (London, 1890), p. 107. The story first appeared as "The Key of the Strong Room" in 1865. See Townley Searle, *Sir William Schwenck Gilbert: A Topsy-Turvy Adventure* (London, 1931), p. 86.
3. See *Fun* (April 2, 1864), 30.
4. *Patience*, in *The Savoy Operas*, Introduction by David Cecil and Notes by Derek Hudson, I (London, 1962), 187. Unless otherwise noted, page references for quotations from the operas are for this edition.
5. "An Autobiography," p. 217.
6. See E. A. Parry's article on Gilbert in *The Dictionary of National Biography*, Second Supplement, II (London, 1912), 107.
7. Jane Stedman, "W. S. Gilbert: His Comic Techniques and Their Development," Unpublished Ph. D. dissertation (Chicago, 1956), p. 7.
8. *The Times*, Oct. 3, 1860, p. 11. The letter has been reprinted in *The Gilbert and Sullivan Journal*, VIII (Jan., 1961), 44.
9. Hesketh Pearson, *Gilbert: His Life and Strife* (London, 1957), p. 51. Quotations by permission of the Hesketh Pearson Estate.
10. *Ibid.*, p. 137.
11. *Ibid.*, p. 44.
12. *Ibid.*, p. 29.
13. Quoted in Gilbert's *Letter Addressed to the Members of the Dramatic Profession in Reply to Miss Henrietta Hodson's Pamphlet* (London, 1877), p. 15. Her pamphlet and Gilbert's *Reply* are both in the Lilly Library at Indiana University.
14. See Pearson, p. 150.
15. *Reply* . . . , p. 15.
16. See Pearson, pp. 137 - 38.
17. *Ibid.*, p. 82.
18. *Ibid.*, p. 167.
19. *Ibid.*, p. 47.

20. *Ibid.*, p. 48. Gilbert's quarrels with critics are interestingly examined by David W. Cole, "The Policy of Contentiousness: Some Non-Literary Factors Contributing to Gilbert's Theatrical Success," in *Gilbert and Sullivan: Papers Presented at the International Conference held at the University of Kansas in May 1970,* James Helyar, ed. (Lawrence, Kansas, 1971), pp. 25 - 31.

21. "Now I've Got You, You Son of a Bitch" is analyzed by Berne in *Games People Play: The Psychology of Human Relationships* (New York, 1964), pp. 84 - 86.

22. In no published letter did Sullivan admit that his affidavit was sworn in ignorance of the facts that Gilbert had uncovered. See Pearson, pp. 148 - 50.

23. Northrop Frye, *Anatomy of Criticism,* First published in 1957 (New York, 1967), p. 166.

24. See A. H. Godwin, *Gilbert and Sullivan; A Critical Appreciation of the Savoy Operas* (London, 1927), p. 89.

25. For a brilliant fictional account of how Victorian proprieties might affect a young gentleman in this decade, see the novel by John Fowles, *The French Lieutenant's Woman* (Boston, 1969).

26. H. Meilhac and Ludovic Halevy, *Les Brigands,* English adaptation by W. S. Gilbert, Act. I (London, 1871).

27. Act III, from the typescript in the Reginald Allen Collection at the Pierpont Morgan Library.

28. From the typescript in the Pierpont Morgan Library.

29. Act III (The phrase is her husband's.).

30. Henri Bergson, "Laughter," in *Comedy,* Wylie Sypher, ed. (New York, 1956), p. 112.

31. *Ibid.*, p. 73.

32. *Ibid.*, p. 89.

33. The date of his first contributions to *Fun* remains uncertain since no one has found a proprietor's copy for any issues before May 27, 1865. See John Bush Jones, "W. S. Gilbert's Contributions to *Fun,* 1865 - 1874," *Bulletin of the New York Public Library,* LXXIII (April, 1969), 253.

34. See Pearson, p. 19, who reports the boot throwing incident as if he had read of it in a letter instead of a story, and Leslie Baily, *The Gilbert and Sullivan Book,* Revised edition, 1956 (London, 1966), p. 46. Neither mentions the fact that F. C. Burnand reports that a boot was thrown at *him* when he was a barrister: see *Records and Reminiscences, Personal and General,* I (London, 1904), 392.

35. "My Maiden Brief," *Cornhill Magazine,* VIII, 728. Subsequent page references appear in the text.

36. Bergson, p. 89.

37. For bibliographical information about Gilbert's early journalism, see the above article by Jones and his dissertation, "The Uncollected Verse of W. S. Gilbert: a Critical edition" (Northwestern, 1969); see also the disserta-

tion by Edward Stewart Lauterbach, "*Fun* and its Contributors: A Literary History of a Victorian Humor Magazine" (Illinois, 1961). Earlier works by Searle, cited above, and Arthur E. Du Bois, "Additions to the Bibliography of W. S. Gilbert's Contributions to Magazines," *Modern Language Notes*, XLVII (1932), 308 - 14, contain more attributions. For corrections of their listings and those by other bibliographers of Gilbert's elusive journalism, see the studies by Jones and the attractive new edition, *The Bab Ballads*, James Ellis, ed. (Cambridge, Mass., 1970).

38. "Maxwell and I," in *Foggerty's Fairy* . . . , pp. 175 - 76.

39. See Charles E. Lauterbach, "Taking Gilbert's Measure," *Huntington Library Quarterly*, LXIX (1956), 196 - 202.

40. See Jones, "W. S. Gilbert's Contributions to *Fun*, 1865 - 1874," p. 253.

41. Hippolyte Taine, *Notes on England*, Edward Hyams, trans. (London, 1957), p. 36.

42. "Men We Meet," *Fun* (May 18, 1867), p. 165.

43. "Club Snobs, II," *Contributions to "Punch"*, *Works*, Biographical Edition, VI (New York, 1898), 439.

44. See "Thumbnail Studies of the London Streets," *London Society*, XII (Oct., 1869), 368.

45. Ellis counts back to "The Story of Gentle Archibald" (May 19, 1866), the first of the poems with "Bab" illustrations; but it strikes me as a less definite beginning, partly because it is in couplets instead of regular stanzas, and also because over a year's lapse occurs between it and "General John."

46. Reprinted in Ellis's edition, p. 65.

47. The existence of this poem has been called to my attention by John Bush Jones, who reprints it and gives an account of its unusual textual history in his dissertation, cited above. See also Ellis's edition, where it appears with notes.

48. *The Savage Club Papers*, Andrew Halliday, ed. (London, 1867), p. 195.

49. *The Mikado*, Act II: *The Savoy Operas*, II, 54.

50. *The Three Clerks*, first published in 1858, Algar Thorold, ed. (London, 1904), p. 172.

51. See Anon., "English History" in *The Annual Register: A Review of Public Events at Home and Abroad, for the Year 1867* (London, 1868), p. 113.

52. Thomas Carlyle, *Macmillan's Magazine*, XVI (August, 1867), 231. See also Michael Wolff, "The Uses of Context: Aspects of the 1860's," *Victorian Studies*, IX (Sept., 1965), 49.

53. John Ruskin, "The Roots of Honour," *Unto This Last*, *The Works of John Ruskin*, E. T. Cook and Alexander Wedderburn, eds., XVII (London, 1905), 32.

54. *Ibid.*, p. 42.

55. Anon., "Mr. Ruskin Again," *Saturday Review*, LXXX (Nov., 1860), 582.

56. Anon., "Political Economy in the Clouds," *Fraser's Magazine*, LXXX (Nov., 1860), 655.

57. See Edith Browne, *W. S. Gilbert* (London, 1907), p. 38; cited in Stedman, p. 300.

58. See Jones, "The Uncollected Verse of W. S. Gilbert . . . ," p. 294.

59. March 1, 1870, *The Swinburne Letters*, Cecil Y. Lang, ed., II (New Haven, 1959), 106.

60. Chesterton, "Every single Savoy Opera is a spoilt Bab Ballad": "Gilbert and Sullivan," in *The Eighteen-Eighties; Essays by Fellows of the Royal Society of Literature*, Walter de la Mare, ed. (Cambridge, England, 1930), p. 145.

Chapter Two

1. Anon., "Two Victorian Humorists: Burnand and the Mask of Gilbert," *Times Literary Supplement* (Nov. 21, 1936), p. 936.

2. Pearson, *Gilbert: His Life and Strife*, p. 20.

3. *Fun*, July 6, 1867, p. 173.

4. Act II, *Princess Toto*, Comic Opera in Three Acts (London, 1876).

5. Gilbert, "Thumbnail Sketches: Getting Up a Pantomime," *London Society*, XIII (Jan. 1868), 50.

6. William Makepeace Thackeray, "Sketches and Travels in London: A Night's Pleasure, III," *Works*, Biographical Edition, VI, 571.

7. See Stedman, "W. S. Gilbert: His Comic Techniques and Their Development," p. 24ff.

8. Thackeray, p. 573.

9. Charles Baudelaire, "On the Essence of Laughter," in *The Comic in Theory and Practice*, John J. Enck, Elizabeth T. Forter, and Alvin Whitely, eds. (New York, 1960), p. 27.

10. See Alexander Bain, *The Emotions and the Will*, First Edition 1859 (New York, D. 1888), pp. 260 - 61.

11. See "On Pantomimic Unities, No. 2," *Fun* (Mar. 26, 1864), p. 13; reprinted by Sidney Dark and Rowland Grey (pseud.), *W. S. Gilbert, His Life and Letters* (London, 1923), pp. 18 ff.

12. Gilbert, "A Consistent Pantomime," *Graphic*, XI (Jan. 16, 1875), 62.

13. Gilbert's pantomime of 1867 - 1868, *Harlequin Cock-Robin and Jenny Wren*, at least partially illustrates his concern with everyday realities: the opening has an anti-pollution motif, with Demon Miasma combatting the Fairy Fresh Air.

14. See *A Stage Play*, William Archer, ed. (New York, 1916), pp. 15 - 16. Gilbert wrote this sketch for Tom Hood's *Comic Annual* of 1873.

15. See the cartoon accompanying the mischievous review in *Punch*, XCV (Dec. 22, 1888), 293. See also Martin Meisal, *Shaw and the Nineteenth Century Theatre* (Princeton, 1963), p. 324.

16. Gilbert, *Original Plays*, Fourth Series (New York, n.d.), p. 31. Ellis discusses the early influence of the pantomime in his introduction to *The Bab Ballads;* see p. 20.

17. "A Consistent Pantomime," *Graphic*, XI, 62.

18. "From Our Stall," *Fun* (May 27, 1865) p. 13.

19. While the Proprietor's Copy is missing for this number, John Jones assumes that this parody is by Gilbert: see "W. S. Gilbert's Contributions to *Fun*," p. 265.

20. Gilbert, "Maud's Peril," *Fun*, Dec. 7, 1867, p. 129.

21. See *Gilbert before Sullivan; Six Comic Plays*, Jane Stedman, ed. (Chicago, 1967) p. 22.

22. *Graphic*, III (Feb. 11, 1871), 135. The Victorian reviews cited in this study are unsigned unless otherwise noted.

23. Stedman, *Gilbert before Sullivan*, p. 48.

24. Ellis cites the failure of what apparently was Gilbert's first professionally performed play, *Uncle Baby* (1863): See Ellis's edition of *The Bab Ballads*, p. 8.

25. See *New and Original Extravaganzas*, Isaac Goldberg, ed. (Boston, 1931), p. x. Page references in the text are to this edition.

26. See Harley Granville-Barker, "Exit Planché — enter Gilbert," *London Mercury*, XXV (March, 1932), 460ff.

27. "The Theatrical Lounger," XII (March 28, 1868) 202. Since Gilbert supposedly began writing for the *Illustrated Times* in 1868, there is a remote possibility that he wrote this review.

28. *The Bohemian Girl*, Osbourne McConathy, ed. (Boston, n.d.), p. 121.

29. *New and Original Extravaganzas*, Goldberg, ed., p. 117.

30. *His Excellency, Original Plays*, Fourth Series, pp. 104 - 105.

31. *An Old Score* (London, 1869), p. 24. See also my essay on "The Affront to Victorian Dignity in the Satire of the Eighteen-Seventies," in *The Nineteenth-Century Writer and His Audience*, Harold Orel and George J. Worth, eds., University of Kansas Humanistic Studies, No. 40, (Lawrence, 1969), p. 107.

32. See "The Idea of Comedy," *The Works of George Meredith*, Memorial Edition, XXVII (London, 1911), 256.

33. "Drama," *Examiner*, (April 28, 1877), 535.

34. See Granville-Barker "Exit Planché — Enter Gilbert," pp. 571 - 72.

35. Stedman, *Gilbert before Sullivan*, p. 5.

36. *Ibid.*, pp. 17ff.

37. See *ibid.*, p. 35. Page references to the German Reed plays are to this edition.

38. I have dealt with this point in "The Affront to Victorian Dignity . . . ," p. 107.

39. See *Gilbert before Sullivan*, p. 35.

40. Joseph Conrad, *Lord Jim*, First edition, 1900, Morton Dauwen Zabel, ed. (Boston, 1958), p. 7.

41. Joseph Conrad, *Nostromo,* First edition, 1904, Foreword by F.R. Leavis (New York, 1960), p. 178.

42. See review in *Graphic,* I (Jan. 15, 1870), 16.

43. "The Theatrical Lounger," *Illustrated Times,* XVI (Jan. 15, 1870), 39.

44. Review in *Graphic,* II (Nov. 26, 1870), 523.

45. Archer, *English Dramatists of Today* (London, 1882) p. 164.

46. *The Palace of Truth, Original Plays,* First Series, p. 189. According to the "Theatrical Lounger," the actor played this part with great success, preserving "all his gush" while "saying the rudest things imaginable." *Illustrated Times,* XVII (Nov. 26, 1870), 343.

47. From "Daphne et Pandrose," quoted in the same issue of the *Illustrated Times* that contains the review of *The Palace of Truth,* Nov. 26, 1870, 343.

48. *Tales of the Castle; or, Stories of Instruction and Delight,* Thomas Holcroft, trans., IV (London, 1819), 192.

49. *The Palace of Truth,* Act II (London, n.d.), p. 34.

50. *Pygmalion and Galatea, Original Plays,* First Series, p. 65.

51. *Broken Hearts, Original Plays,* Second Series, p. 7.

52. Gilbert's Letter of Dec. 6, 1875, typescript in Pierpont Morgan Library; quoted by Pearson in *Gilbert: His Life and Strife,* p. 47.

53. "Mr. Gilbert's Plays" (by "T. W."), *Examiner,* April 22, 1876, pp. 461 - 62. A modern reading of Gilbert's plays as allegory has been advanced by Herbert Weisinger, who thinks that Gilbert is deeply indebted to *The Faerie Queene:* see "The Twisted Cue," in *The Agony and the Triumph: Papers on the Use and Abuse of Myth* (East Lansing, 1964).

54. *Original Plays,* Second Series, p. 98.

55. *Original Plays,* First Series, p. 105.

56. See review in *Graphic,* IX (Jan. 10, 1874), 38.

57. See Dame Madge Kendal, "W. S. Gilbert," *Cornhill Magazine,* CXLVIII (Sept., 1933), 308 - 309.

58. Annie Edwards, *Ought We to Visit Her?* (New York, 1871), p. 128.

59. *Original Plays,* Second Series, p. 186.

60. Gilbert's letter to E. Bruce Hindle (Jan. 29, 1885), typescript in the Pierpont Morgan Library.

61. *Original Plays,* Second Series, p. 214.

62. *Original Plays,* Second Series, p. 84.

63. *Academy,* XII (27 Oct. 1877), 416.

64. *Original Plays,* Second Series, p. 126.

65. *The Dolmen Boucicault,* David Krause, ed. (Dublin, 1964), p. 104.

66. 105 performances, according to Leslie Baily, p. 134.

67. Quoted in Baily, pp. 134 - 35.

68. *Original Plays,* Third Series, p. 86.

69. See "At the Play," *Theatre,* I (Aug. 1, 1878), 65.

70. *The Times,* Oct. 8, 1877, p. 11.

71. *Examiner,* Oct. 20, 1877, p. 1336.

72. *Athenaeum,* Oct. 13, 1874, p. 475.

73. *Illustrated London News,* LXXI (Oct. 13, 1877), 363.

74. Augustin Filon, *The English Stage, Being an Account of the Victorian Drama,* Fred. Whyte, trans. (London, 1897), p. 146.

75. *The Times,* August 11, 1875, p. 9. The context of this editorial is given in the informative dissertation by Randolph M. Bulgin, "Anthony Trollope's *The Way We Live Now:* A Study in Its Historical Background and Critical Significance" (Princeton, 1963).

76. Anthony Trollope, *Autobiography,* Preface by Frederick Page (London, 1950), p. 353.

77. "Belles Lettres," *Westminster Review,* CIV (Oct., 1875), 257. Bulgin analyzes the response to this novel.

78. *Diaries of Lewis Carroll,* Roger L. Green, ed., II (London, 1953), 369.

79. *The Times,* Oct. 8, 1877, p. 11.

80. *Academy,* XII (Oct. 27, 1877), 416.

81. *Saturday Review,* XLIV (Oct. 13, 1877), 455.

82. Shaw's letter to William Archer (April 23, 1894), *Bernard Shaw: Collected Letters, 1874 - 1897,* Dan H. Laurence, ed. (New York, 1965), p. 427.

83. "Drama," *Examiner,* Oct. 20, 1877, p. 1336.

84. "The Phantom Head," *Fun,* Dec. 19, 1868, p. 151.

Chapter Three

1. See Baily, p. 44.

2. Edward Stewart Lauterbach assumes that the monogram is Gilbert's: see "*Fun* and its Contributors," pp. 91 - 92.

3. "Our Own Correspondent at 'Orphée aux Enfers'," *Fun* (Dec. 24, 1864), p. 148. The attribution lacks definite proof, but Gilbert was at least illustrating "Our Own Correspondent" in 1864, and he surely must have written "Our Own Correspondent Called to the Bar" (Dec. 3, 1864), p. 118.

4. See Baily, p. 323.

5. "The Theatrical Lounger," *Illustrated Times,* XIV (Jan. 2, 1868), 7. See also François Cellier and Cunningham Bridgeman, *Gilbert and Sullivan and Their Operas,* (Boston, 1914), p. 38, for more evidence of Gilbert's musical tastes.

6. "From Our Stall," *Fun,* June 1, 1867, pp. 128 - 30; quoted in Reginald Allen's *W. S. Gilbert: An Anniversary Survey and Exhibition Checklist* (Charlottesville, Va., 1963), p. 6.

7. See Pearson, *Gilbert: His Life and Strife,* p. 255.

8. "The Precocious Baby" was the ballad Gilbert used in *No Cards.*

9. Reprinted in Ellis's edition of *The Bab Ballads,* "Trial by Jury" appeared in *Fun,* April 11, 1868, p. 54.

10. See Chapter 1, Part III.

11. David Cecil, *The Savoy Operas*, I, xvii.

12. Stedman, *Gilbert Before Sullivan*, p. 30.

13. "The Theatrical Lounger," *Illustrated Times*, XV (Nov. 27, 1869), 343.

14. See Terence Rees, *Thespis, A Gilbert & Sullivan Enigma* (London, 1964), p. 64.

15. Stedman, *Gilbert Before Sullivan*, p. 30.

16. Clennell Wilkinson, "Gilbert and Sullivan," *London Mercury*, V (March, 1922), 501. See also the interesting chapter by Gervase Hughes on "Rhythm and Word Setting" in *The Music of Arthur Sullivan* (New York, 1960).

17. See Baily, p. 84.

18. *Ibid.*, p. 144.

19. *Ibid.*, p. 323.

20. F. M. Cornford, *The Origin of Attic Comedy* (London, 1914), p. 18. See also Walter Sichel, "The English Aristophanes," *Fortnightly Review*, XCVI (Oct. 2, 1911), 681 - 704; and Edith Hamilton, "W. S. Gilbert: A Mid-Victorian Aristophanes," *Theatre Arts Monthly*, XI (Oct., 1927), 781 - 90.

21. See Stedman's chapter on "Gilbert's Double Worlds" in her dissertation, "W. S. Gilbert: His Comic Techniques and Their Development."

22. See Cornford, pp. 132ff.

23. Edward Bulwer Lytton, *England and the English*, II (London, 1833), 141.

24. "The Happy Land," *Graphic*, VII (Mar. 8, 1873), 219.

25. Translated by Edith Hamilton in "W. S. Gilbert: A Mid-Victorian Aristophanes," p. 788. For a recent study of this work see Elwood P. Lawrence, *"The Happy Land:* W. S. Gilbert as Political Satirist," *Victorian Studies*, XV (1971), 161 - 83.

26. In addition to Archer's view in *English Dramatists of Today*, p. 180, see Wilkinson, p. 504 and Arthur E. DuBois, "W. S. Gilbert, Practical Classicist," *Sewanee Review*, XXXVII (Jan., 1929), 104. See also Dean Burton Farnsworth's objection to this view in "Satire in the Works of W. S. Gilbert," Ph. D. dissertation, (University of California, 1950), p. 8.

27. Quoted in Baily, p. 149.

28. See Hesketh Pearson, *Dizzy: The Life and Personality of Benjamin Disraeli, Earl of Beaconsfield* (New York, 1951), p. 278.

29. Dark and Grey, p. 229. Cecil's view is expressed in *The Savoy Operas*, I, x.

30. *Academy*, XXXVI (Dec. 14, 1889), 395.

31. See *London Music in 1888 - 89* in *The Works of Bernard Shaw*, XXXIII (London, 1938) 250 - 51; *Music in London, 1890 - 94* in *Works*, XXVI, 124; for the review of *Utopia*, see *Works*, XXVIII, 61 - 66.

32. See review in *Fun*, (April 4, 1874), p. 145.

33. *Topsy-Turvydom*, typescript in Pierpont Morgan Library. The play was privately printed by the Oxford University Press in 1931.

34. *The Happy Land* (London, 1873), p. 12.

35. G. Wilson Knight, *The Golden Labyrinth: A Study of British Drama* (London, 1962), p. 302.

36. See Philip Magnus, *Gladstone, A Biography* (New York, 1954), p. 249.

37. See the editorial in *Graphic*, XVII (Mar. 2, 1878), 210.

38. See Baily, p. 155, who cites a possible source for this song in Dickens' *Martin Chuzzlewit*.

39. See Ashley H. Thorndike, *English Comedy* (New York, 1929), p. 557.

40. See Baily, p. 343.

41. See Louis Kronenberger's *Thread of Laughter: Chapters on English Stage Comedy from Jonson to Maugham*, (New York, 1952), p. 206; and Kresh's "Confessions of a Gilbert and Sullivan Addict; or, The Unrepentant Savoyard," *Hi-Fi/Stereo Review*, February, 1967; with excerpts reprinted in the January and May, 1968, issues of *The Savoyard*.

42. See Baily, p. 406.

43. See Cellier and Bridgeman, p. 130.

44. See Gerardus Van der Leeuw, *Sacred and Profane Beauty: The Holy in Art*, David E. Green, trans. (New York, 1965), p. 77: "Drama . . . consists of movement and countermovement."

45. See Cornford, p. 38.

46. *Anatomy of Criticism*, p. 46.

47. See Barbara Tuchman's chapter on Richard Strauss in *The Proud Tower: A Portrait of the World Before the War, 1890 - 1914* (New York, 1966). Gilbert's interest in the macabre at this point in his career is also shown by the fact that he considered basing a comic opera on *Frankenstein* after *The Mikado*; see Donald A. Reed, "Gothic Gilbert and Sullivan?" *Gilbert and Sullivan Journal*, VIII (Sept., 1962), 120.

48. Derek Hudson offers a rough English equivalent to the Japanese: "O! he was frightened to death!" *Savoy Operas*, II, 34. Subsequent quotations of the operas, unless noted otherwise, are from this edition.

49. See James D. Ellis, "The Comic Vision of W. S. Gilbert," Ph. D. dissertation (State University of Iowa, 1964), p. 338.

50. See Audrey Williamson, *Gilbert and Sullivan Opera: A New Assessment* (London, 1953), p. 143.

51. *Gilbert Before Sullivan*, p. 126.

52. See Knight, p. 302.

53. *Original Plays*, Second Series, p. 57.

54. Phyllis Karr has questioned the propriety of calling Gilbert's characters "puppets" in a paper read at the International Conference on Gilbert and Sullivan: the title is "Character Development of Robin Oakapple, or Being Cursed is Good for a Fellow."

55. See Williamson, p. 115.

56. *Iolanthe* Notebook, p. 16, Pierpont Morgan Library. See also Baily, p. 226 ff.

57. See Cyril Rollins and R. John Witts, *The D'Oyly Carte Opera Com-*

pany in *Gilbert and Sullivan Operas: A Record of Productions 1875 - 1961* (London, 1962), p. 1.

58. Quoted by Herbert Sullivan and Newman Flower, *Sir Arthur Sullivan: His Life, Letters, and Diaries* (New York, 1927), p. 237.

59. Sullivan's Symphony in E minor and the Overture "Di Ballo," performed by the Royal Liverpool Philharmonic Orchestra, were recorded in 1968 by The Gramophone Company, Ltd.

60. See Baily, p. 327.

61. *Ibid.*

62. *Ibid.*, p. 328.

63. *Ibid.*

64. *Ibid.*, p. 329.

65. *Ibid.*, p. 330.

66. See Cyril Rollins and R. John Witts, p. 1.

67. Hughes speaks appreciatively of Cellier's score in *The Music of Arthur Sullivan*, p. 22. A complete recording of *The Mountebanks* was released by the Lyric Theatre Company of Washington, D.C., in the 1960's.

68. See Thomas E. Dunhill, *Sullivan's Comic Operas: A Critical Appreciation* (New York, 1928), p. 211.

69. See Shaw, *Music in London, 1890 - 94, Works*, XXVIII, 63.

70. See Herbert Sullivan and Newman Flower, p. 222. A long-awaited D'Oyly Carte recording of highlights from *Utopia* shows that Sullivan's talents were still vital.

71. Review in *Fun* (Mar. 17, 1896), p. 102.

72. Review in *Graphic*, LIII (March 14, 1896), 315.

73. Edmond W. Rickett and Benjamin T. Hoogland, *Let's Do Some Gilbert and Sullivan: A Practical Production Handbook* (New York, 1940), p. 123. Complete recordings of *Utopia* and *The Grand Duke* were released by the Lyric Theatre Company of Washington, D.C., in the 1960's; a complete performance of the later opera has been recorded, live, by the Mount Oread Gilbert and Sullivan Company of Lawrence, Kansas, in 1970.

74. See John Bush Jones, "Gilbertian Humor: Pulling Together a Definition," *Victorian Newsletter* (Spring, 1968), pp. 28 - 31.

75. Pearson, *Gilbert and Sullivan* (New York, 1935), 219. The duet is quoted from *Original Plays*, Third Series (London, 1895), p. 387.

76. Sypher, *Comedy*, p. 197.

77. Baily, p. 227.

78. *Utopia* Notebook, Pierpont Morgan Library, pp. 5 - 6.

79. See "Chronicle," *Annual Register for 1891*, p. 16.

80. See "Court Martial of Vice Admiral Fairfax," *Graphic*, XLVII (Jan. 7, 1893), 4, 6.

81. "Chronicle," *Annual Register for 1893*, p. 39.

82. See Charles Petrie, *The Victorians* (New York, 1962), pp. 63 - 65.

83. Quoted in Baily, p. 379.

84. Reginald Allen, ed., *The First Night Gilbert and Sullivan: Containing*

Complete Librettos of the Fourteen Operas, Exactly as Presented at Their Première Performances . . . (New York, 1958), p. 413.

85. Gilbert's phrase in a letter of March 9, 1896, to Mrs. Bram Stoker; quoted in Allen, *W. S. Gilbert: An Anniversary Survey*, p. 68.

86. For an account of the growing number of political assassinations near the turn of the century, see Tuchman's *Proud Tower*, pp. 63 ff.

87. See Sypher, p. 221.

88. See the interesting letter by Jonathan Strong, Jr., on using a small stage upon the stage in a production of this opera: *Gilbert and Sullivan Journal*, VII (Jan., 1964).

Chapter Four

1. "The Hooligan," *Century Magazine*, LXXXIII (Nov., 1911), 99. Page reference will be to this text.

2. Edith Browne, *W. S. Gilbert*, p. 40.

3. *The First Night Gilbert and Sullivan*, Reginald Allen, ed. p. 199.

4. Samuel Hynes, *The Edwardian Turn of Mind* (Princeton, 1968), p. 6.

5. See Pearson, *Gilbert: His Life and Strife*, p. 237.

6. Gilbert's letter to Alfred Austin, Dec. 14, 1889, typescript in Pierpont Morgan Library.

7. Pearson, *Gilbert and Sullivan*, p. 294.

8. Shaw, *Our Theatres in the Nineties, Works*, XXIV, 242; see also Shaw's reference to *The Pirates of Penzance* in the preface to *Man and Superman*.

9. Shaw, *Music in the Nineties, Works*, XXVI, 238. See also Ellis's dissertation, p 228ff.

10. Shaw's letter to William Archer, April 23, 1894, *Collected Letters, 1874 - 1897*, p. 427.

11. *Arms and the Man*, Act III, in *Plays Pleasant and Unpleasant, Works*, VIII, 64.

12. "Preface" to the Second Volume of *Plays Pleasant and Unpleasant, Works*, VIII, xvi.

13. Anon., "The Revolutionary Satire of W. S. Gilbert," *Littell's Living Age*, CCCXI (Dec. 24, 1921), 795; first published in *Looking Forward, A Monthly Review of World Movements*, (Nov., 1921).

14. *Ibid.*, p. 798.

15. *The Letters of Rupert Brooke*, Geoffrey Keynes, ed. (London, 1969), p. 365.

Selected Bibliography

BIBLIOGRAPHIES

No definitive bibliography of Gilbert's work exists, but the following studies cover the bulk of it.

ALLEN, REGINALD. *W. S. Gilbert: An Anniversary Survey and Exhibition Checklist with Thirty-Five Illustrations.* Charlottesville, Virginia: Bibliographical Society of the University of Virginia, 1963. Exceptionally comprehensive in listing the dramatic works.

DuBois, ARTHUR E. "Additions to the Bibliography of W. S. Gilbert's Contributions to Magazines." *Modern Language Notes,* XLVII (May, 1932), 308 - 14. An early attempt to supplement and correct the work of Townley Searle.

ELLIS, JAMES. "Bibliography" in "The Comic Vision of W. S. Gilbert." Unpublished Dissertation. State University of Iowa, 1964. Lists Gilbert's dramatic works and some of his journalistic writing.

JONES, JOHN BUSH. "W. S. Gilbert's Contributions to *Fun,* 1865 - 1874." *Bulletin of the New York Public Library,* LXXIII (April, 1969), 253 - 66. Attributions based on the Proprietor's Copy; chronological listing, with a brief indication of the nature of each contribution.

SEARLE, TOWNLEY. *Sir William Schwenck Gilbert: A Topsy-turvy Adventure.* Introduction by R. E. Swartwout. London: Alexander-Ouseley, 1931. Sometimes unreliable and incomplete in its information, this study is still useful in showing the range of Gilbert's writing.

PRIMARY SOURCES

Collections
Verse and Stories
The Bab Ballads, Much Sound and Little Sense. London: John Camden Hotten, 1869.
The Bab Ballads, with which are included Songs of a Savoyard. London: George Routledge and Sons, 1898.
ELLIS, JAMES, ed. *The Bab Ballads.* Cambridge, Mass.: Belknap Press of Harvard University Press, 1970. Contains almost all of the journalistic

verse that can be identified as Gilbert's. Ellis uses the original il-
lustrations but keeps Gilbert's revisions of the texts in most instances.
An annotated edition.
Foggerty's Fairy and Other Tales. London: George Routledge and Sons,
1890.
JONES, JOHN BUSH, ed. "The Uncollected Verse of W. S. Gilbert: A Critical
Edition." Unpublished Dissertation. Northwestern, 1969.

Dramatic Works
For a virtually complete listing, including unpublished plays, see Allen's *An-
niversary Survey.*
ALLEN, REGINALD, ed. *The First Night Gilbert and Sullivan; Containing
Complete Librettos of the Fourteen Operas, Exactly as Presented at
Their Première Performances. . . .* New York: Limited Editions Club,
1958. Notes variations from later texts and supplies informative in-
troductions dealing with the reception of each opera. Illustrated with
sketches from Victorian periodicals.
GOLDBERG, ISAAC, ed. *New and Original Extravaganzas.* Boston: John W.
Luce, 1931.
HUDSON, DEREK, ed. *The Savoy Operas,* I. Introduction by David Cecil.
London: Oxford University Press, 1962.
————. *The Savoy Operas,* II. Introduction by Bridget D'Oyly Carte. Lon-
don: Oxford University Press, 1963. The texts of these two volumes
are supposed to reflect Gilbert's alterations.
Original Plays, First Series. London: Chatto and Windus, 1925.
Original Plays, Second Series. London: Chatto and Windus, 1922.
Original Plays, Third Series. London: Chatto and Windus, 1911.
Original Plays, Fourth Series. London: Chatto and Windus, 1911.
STEDMAN, JANE, ed. *Gilbert Before Sullivan: Six Comic Plays.* Chicago:
University of Chicago Press, 1967. Offers a full historical and critical
introduction, illustrations, helpful annotations, and even Frederic
Clay's music for *Ages Ago.*

Uncollected Miscellaneous Prose
The following list is a sampling of Gilbert's uncollected journalism. Only a
few of Gilbert's contributions to *Fun* are included: those beginning with
May 20, 1865 are listed in Jones' article, cited above. Most of the informa-
tion for what does appear comes from Searle, Ellis, and the Gilbert collection
in the Lilly Library.
"An Appeal to the Press." *Era Almanack, 1878.* London, pp. 85 - 86.
"An Autobiography." *Theatre,* N. S. I (April 2, 1883), 217 - 24.
"The Brigands." *Era,* LII (Nov. 9, 1889), 9.
"The Comic Physiognomist." *Fun.* First Series begins November 3, 1863,
and ends February 27, 1864; Second Series begins May 21, 1864, and
ends August 6, 1864. Resumed in February, 1867, as "Men We
Meet."

"A Consistent Pantomime." *Graphic*, XI (Jan. 16, 1875), 62 - 63.

"Emily and Augusta." *Tom Hood's Comic Annual, 1870*. London: [1869]. Pp. 95 - 98. Illustrations with captions.

"From St. Paul's to Piccadilly." *Belgravia*, II (1867), 67 - 74.

"The History of a Gentleman Who Was Born at an Advanced Age." *The Five Alls (Warne's Christmas Annual)*. Tom Hood, ed. London: Frederick Warne, [1866]. Pp. 84 - 85.

"Honours of the Shrievalty." *London Society*, VII (May, 1865), 410 - 15.

"A Hornpipe in Fetters." *Era Almanack, 1879*. London. Pp. 91 - 92.

"Johnson; or, He Is Your Brother." *Tom Hood's Comic Annual, 1868*. London: [1867]. Pp. 93 - 95. Miniature burlesque drama.

"Jones' Victoria Cross." *Once a Week*, IV (Nov. 2, 1867), 530 - 33.

"The Lady in the Plaid Shawl." *The Flag* (The Book of the Union Jack Club). H. F. Trippel, ed. London: *Daily Mail*, [1908]. Pp. 25 - 33.

"The Lawyer's Story." *The Five Alls (Warne's Christmas Annual)*. Tom Hood, ed. London: Frederick Warne, [1866]. Pp. 35 - 36.

Notebooks: "*Iolanthe* Notebook," "*Utopia* Notebook." Unpublished; in the Reginald Allen Collection of the Pierpont Morgan Library.

"On the Cards — Diamonds." *Routledge's Christmas Annual, 1867*. E. Routledge, ed. London: Routledge and Sons, [1866]. Pp. 25 - 37.

"On Pantomimic Unities." *Fun*, (Feb. 20, 1864), p. 230; (March 26, 1864), p. 13.

"Our Critic Among the Pictures." *Fun* (June 18, 1864), pp. 133 - 34.

"Our Own Correspondent Out for a Holiday." *Fun*, (August 13, 1864), through Sept. 3, 1864). Attributed to Gilbert on basis of drawings signed "W. S. G." and style.

The Pinafore Picture Book. Illustrated by Alice B. Woodward. London: George Bell and Sons, 1908.

"Mr. Pip and Mr. Pop; or, the Two Stock Brokers," *Tom Hood's Comic Annual, 1868*. London: [1867]. Pp. 100 - 101. Illustrated story foreshadowing O. Henry's "Ransom of Red Chief."

"A Proposal for Elevating the Position of the Modern Drama." *Era Almanack, 1875*. London. Pp. 86 - 87.

"The Recent Hideous Case of Hydrophobia." *Punch*, (July 29, 1865), p. 35. Illustration signed "Bab."

The Story of the Mikado. Illustrated by Alice B. Woodward. London: Daniel O'Connor, 1921.

"Thumbnail Studies: Getting Up a Pantomime." *London Society*, XIII (Jan., 1868), 50 - 57.

"Thumbnail Studies in the London Streets." *London Society*, XII (Aug., 1867), 224 - 27; (Oct., 1867), 368 - 72; (Dec., 1867), 557 - 62.

"Thumbnail Studies: Sitting at a Play." *London Society*, XIII (Feb., 1868), 132 - 36.

"A Wonderful Shillingsworth." *Punch*, (Dec. 16, 1865), p. 236. (Signed "Bab".)

SECONDARY SOURCES

This selected listing does not include articles collected in *W. S. Gilbert: A Century of Scholarship and Commentary* or in *Gilbert and Sullivan: Papers* . . . (cited below). A fuller bibliography of studies published before 1964 is found in the dissertation by James Ellis.

Books and Articles

ANONYMOUS. "The Revolutionary Satire of W. S. Gilbert." *Littel's Living Age*, CCCXI (Dec. 24, 1921), 795 - 98. Eccentric thesis, in radical contrast with the popular view in the 1920's that Gilbert did not write true satire.

———. "Two Victorian Humorists: Burnand and the Mask of Gilbert," *Times Literary Supplement*, Nov. 21, 1936, pp. 935 - 36. Outlines Gilbert's way of exploring the mind of his era.

BAILY, LESLIE. *The Gilbert and Sullivan Book*. Revised edition, 1956. London: Spring Books, 1966. Fully illustrated, lively account of the careers of both partners, with much information about productions.

———. *Gilbert and Sullivan and Their World*. London: Thames and Hudson, 1973. Condensed historical survey of their careers, with fine illustrations.

BROWNE, EDITH A. *W. S. Gilbert*. London: John Lane, 1907. Biographical study; based partly on conversations with Gilbert.

CELLIER, FRANÇOIS and CUNNINGHAM BRIDGEMAN. *Gilbert and Sullivan and Their Operas*. Boston: Little, Brown, 1914. Lively information about rehearsals and productions in the part by Cellier, the conductor at the Savoy.

CLINTON-BADDELEY, V. C. *The Burlesque Tradition in the English Theatre after 1660*. London: Methuen, 1952. Denies that Gilbert is a satirist.

DARK, SIDNEY and ROWLAND GREY (pseud.). *W. S. Gilbert, His Life and Letters*. London: Methuen, [1923]. Rambling, sometimes inaccurate, but still needed to supplement the work of Hesketh Pearson.

DARLINGTON, W. A. *The World of Gilbert and Sullivan*. New York: Thomas Y. Crowell, 1950. Treats an important topic but does not fully show the pertinence of Gilbert's work to Victorian times.

DUNN, GEORGE E. *A Gilbert and Sullivan Dictionary*. London: G. Allen and Unwin, [1936]. Helpful on topical allusions.

DUNNHILL, THOMAS F. *Sullivan's Comic Operas: A Critical Appreciation*. London, Oxford University Press, 1928. Perceptive appraisal from a musician's viewpoint.

ELLIS, JAMES. "The Comic Vision of W. S. Gilbert." Unpublished Ph. D. dissertation. State University of Iowa, 1964. Thorough analytic study, often from a philosophic point of view.

"E. S. G." "A Savoy Rehearsal." *Graphic*, XLVIII (Oct. 7, 1893), 447 - 50. Detailed report of Gilbert and Sullivan at a late rehearsal of *Utopia Limited*.

FARNSWORTH, DEAN BURTON. "Satire in the Works of W. S. Gilbert." Unpublished Ph. D. dissertation. University of California, 1950. Comprehensive survey of the kinds of Gilbertian satire.

GARSON, R. W. "The English Aristophanes," *Revue de Littérature Comparée*, XLVI (1972), 177 - 93. A sound analysis of Gilbert's right to this title.

GODWIN, A. H. *Gilbert and Sullivan: A Critical Appreciation of the Savoy Opera*. London: J. M. Dent and Sons, 1927. Impressionistic, with some insights.

GOLDBERG, ISAAC. *The Story of Gilbert and Sullivan, or the 'Compleat' Savoyard*. First Edition, 1928. New York: AMS Press, 1970. A copious historical-critical survey, spiced with the anti-Victorian tone of the 1920's.

GRANVILLE-BARKER, HARLEY. "Exit Planché — Enter Gilbert." *London Mercury*, XXV (March, April, 1932), 457 - 66, 558 - 73. Shows Gilbert's contribution to burlesque in the 1860's.

HALTON, FREDERICK J. *The Gilbert and Sullivan Operas: A Concordance*. Foreword by Rupert D'Oyly Carte. New York: Bass Publishers, [1935]. Informative reference book with a few well-chosen photographs.

HEAD, THOMAS GARRETT, JR. "Contract to Please: A Study of the Plays of W. S. Gilbert." Unpublished Ph. D. dissertation. Stanford University, 1970. Perceptive criticism, supported by careful research.

HELYAR, JAMES, ed. *Gilbert and Sullivan: Papers Presented at the International Conference Held at the University of Kansas in May 1970*. Lawrence, Kansas, 1971. Covers a wide range of topics, with major essays by Colin Prestige on Gilbert's reception in the United States and by Jane Stedman on his stagecraft.

HINDLE, E. BRUCE. "W. S. Gilbert, Playwright and Humorist." *Manchester Quarterly*, XLII (Jan., 1885), 55 - 85. Expresses the standard Victorian distress over Gilbert's alleged lack of sympathy; Gilbert responded with a thoughtful but tart letter to Hindle that is now in the Pierpont Morgan Library.

HOW, HARRY. "Illustrated Interviews: Mr. W. S. Gilbert." *Strand Magazine*, II (Oct., 1891), 331 - 41. Photographs document the opulence of Gilbert's life at Grim's Dyke.

HUGHES, GERVASE. *The Music of Arthur Sullivan*. New York: St. Martins Press, 1960. Excellent on the setting of Gilbert's words to music.

JACOBS, ARTHUR. *Gilbert and Sullivan*. London: Max Parrish, 1951. A brief survey, affording insight concerning Sullivan's contribution.

JELLINEK, HEDY and GEORGE. "The One World of Gilbert and Sullivan." *Saturday Review*, (October 26, 1968), pp. 69 - 70, 72, 94. Shows how the operas have penetrated the non-English-speaking parts of the world.

JONES, JOHN BUSH. "Gilbertian Humor: Pulling Together a Definition." *Vic-*

torian Newsletter, (Spring, 1968), pp. 28 - 31. Builds on Archer's views; stresses importance of logic rigidly worked out in fantastic situations.

————, ed. *W. S. Gilbert: A Century of Scholarship and Commentary.* Foreword by Bridget D'Oyly Carte. New York: New York University Press, 1970. Essays ranging from reviews of *The Bab Ballads* to recent bibliographical studies and Stedman's account of the evolution of *Patience* from manuscript notes.

KENDAL, MADGE. "W. S. Gilbert." *Cornhill Magazine,* CXLVIII (Sept., 1933), 303 - 316. An actress's reminiscences of Gilbert as director.

KNIGHT, G. WILSON. *The Golden Labyrinth: A Study of British Drama.* London: Phoenix House, [1962]. Offers stimulating ideas about the vision of life implicit in Gilbert's operas.

LAUTERBACH, EDWARD STEWART. "*Fun* and Its Contributors: A Literary History of a Victorian Humor Magazine." Unpublished Ph. D. dissertation. Illinois, 1961. Provides a detailed context for a survey of Gilbert's comic journalism.

LAWRENCE, ELWOOD P. "*The Happy Land:* W. S. Gilbert as Political Satirist," *Victorian Studies,* XV (1971), 161 - 83. Sees Gilbert as a reactionary satirist.

LIEBMAN, ARTHUR M. "The Works of W. S. Gilbert: A Study of Their Aristophanic Elements and Their Relationship to the Development of the Nineteenth and Twentieth Century British Theatre." Unpublished Ph. D. dissertation. New York University, 1971. Informative comparative study, in cumbersome form.

MANDER, RAYMOND and JOE MITCHENSON. *A Picture History of Gilbert and Sullivan.* London: Vista Books, 1962. Includes photographs of scenes from original productions.

MOORE, FRANK LEDLIE. *Crowell's Handbook of Gilbert and Sullivan.* New York: Thomas Y. Crowell, 1962. Contains bibliographical material, summaries of plots, etc.

PEARSON, HESKETH. *Gilbert and Sullivan, A Biography.* New York: Harper and Brothers, 1935. Readable, but sketchy.

————. *Gilbert: His Life and Strife.* London: Methuen, [1957]. Currently the best biography, but not a definitive one.

REES, TERENCE. *Thespis, A Gilbert and Sullivan Enigma.* London: Dillons University Bookshop, 1964. Finely documented view of the original production.

RICKETT, EDMOND and BENJAMIN T. HOOGLAND. *Let's Do Some Gilbert and Sullivan: A Practical Production Handbook.* New York: Coward-McCann, [1940].

ROLLINS, CYRIL and R. JOHN WITTS. *The D'Oyly Carte Opera Company in Gilbert and Sullivan Operas: A Record of Productions, 1875 - 1961.* London: Michael Joseph, [1962]. Exhaustive statistical record; includes productions by touring companies.

SCOTT, NAN C. "Five Little-Known Operas of Gilbert and Sullivan." M. A. Thesis. University of Kansas, 1965. Analyzes libretti and music from the viewpoint of a director who would consider staging *The Sorcerer, Princess Ida, Ruddigore, Utopia Limited,* and *The Grand Duke.*

SHAW, GEORGE BERNARD. *Our Theatres in the Nineties. The Collected Works of Bernard Shaw.* 33 vols. London: Constable 1930 - 1938. XXII - XXV. Challenging remarks about Gilbert here and in *Music in London.*

STEDMAN, JANE W. "From Dame to Woman: W. S. Gilbert and Theatrical Transvestism." *Victorian Studies,* XIV (Sept., 1970), 27 - 46. Balances the exaggerated accounts of Gilbert's "sadism" in portraying aging women.

————. "W. S. Gilbert: His Comic Techniques and Their Development." Unpublished Ph. D. dissertation. Chicago, 1956. Important for showing Gilbert's place in the Victorian theater and for developing an illuminating view of the conflicts in the operas.

SULLIVAN, HERBERT and NEWMAN FLOWER. *Sir Arthur Sullivan: His Life, Letters, and Diaries.* New York: George H. Doran, [1927]. Contains much information about Gilbert's dealings with the composer.

SUTTON, MAX KEITH. "The Affront to Victorian Dignity in the Satire of the Eighteen-Seventies." *The Nineteenth-Century Writer and His Audience.* Harold Orel and George J. Worth, eds. University of Kansas Humanistic Studies, No. 40. Lawrence: University of Kansas Publications, 1969. Relates Gilbert's to other satire in this decade.

THORNDIKE, ASHLEY H. *English Comedy.* New York: Macmillan, 1929. Finds "the exhilaration of a game" in the operas.

WILLIAMSON, AUDREY. *Gilbert and Sullivan Opera: A New Assessment.* London: Rockliff Publishing Corporation, [1953]. A major study dealing with music and production as well as themes, plots, characters.

YOUNG, PERCY M. *Sir Arthur Sullivan.* London: J. M. Dent & Sons, 1971. A large biographical and critical study; shows the context of the operas from a musicologist's viewpoint.

Periodicals

The American Gilbert and Sullivan Quarterly. New York, 1935 - 38.

The Gilbert and Sullivan Journal. London, 1925 —.

The Savoyard. London, 1962 —.

Index

(The works of Gilbert are listed under his name)